SOME LIKE IT HOT

Some Like It Hot

The Sauna, Its Lore and Stories

Nicolyn Rajala

NORTH STAR PRESS OF ST. CLOUD, INC.

Artwork featured on pages 17 and 25 and the *Sauna Rules* on page 23 used with permissiom of the artist, La Verne Rengo. Reproductions of this artwork and the *Sauna Rules* can be purchased from:

Finnish Designs
178 St. Louis River Road E.
Duluth MN 55810
www.finnishdesigns.com   Fax: 218-628-0211

Contents

Part I
Sauna Basics

Chapter One

In the Beginning
THE FIRST SAUNA

"There they sat, side by side, amidst the steam and enjoyed the pleasure of the fish. Antti was musing: 'D'you think there might be a sauna in heaven?' 'Course there must be,' said Jussi."
Maiju Lassila

On a freezing and stormy night many many years ago, three brothers huddled with their families about their hearth fire in a small roofed pit dug into the steep side of a half-frozen hill. They held their shaking hands out to the meager heat from the yellow flames that sputtered in a circle of large rocks, while smoke wisped into a thick layer over their heads. The adults would not meet the children's eyes, for fear of revealing what everybody thought: they were all going to die. Fire or not, they were trapped in a hastily-made hut, and the great cold would snatch them away, one by one.

The day before, Juha, the youngest brother, had discovered this place for his wife Marjatta, heavily pregnant with their first child. Juha had set to digging while the wives of the older brothers dragged willow saplings over, stripped them of their limbs, and drove them into the earth. Atop this frame they spread large reindeer skins.

Juha's older brothers had hunted, traveling a far distance, and returned with only a small grouse just as the icy rain turned into sleet, then snow whirled by a bitter wind.

1

The first day they shared the bird. After that, there had been only thin broth made from the bones, and now that was gone. Marjatta had been well, but they were concerned about the baby; it would not do to arrive at Marjatta's parents' farm with a dead baby. The cold deepened. The tent kept the wind and icy wetness out, but it could not eliminate the cold that seeped under the reindeer skins to chill them. The fire provided little warmth, and the icy air bored into their bones, until they knew they could not stand much more.

For two days, they huddled in their hut, teeth chattering, as the temperature plummeted. Trees cracked in the cold. The snow and wind roared about them. They sat, waiting for death.

Lasse stirred from his sleep. "Mama, I'm cold" he whined.

His mother handed him the remainder of her steaming cup of weak tea. She cautioned him not to drop the cup, but his small sleepy hand missed its grip and spilled the cup's contents onto the hot fire stones.

"Tsssss," the tea sizzled as it evaporated off the rocks. The frigid smoky air was suddenly filled with the aroma of herbs.

And then something more: the unmistakable sensation of heat!

Marialiisa scolded Lasse. In her anger she was unaware of the rise in temperature in their makeshift tent.

But not the other adults, who lifted their noses to the air, sniffed it, waved their hands through its stunning warmth, flexing their fingers as they glanced at the fallen cup, the hot stones, and the sudden sparks of hope in each other's shining eyes.

The older brother was the first to act. He poured an inch of liquid from a deer bladder into the cup, and then dribbled it gently over the hot fire stones.

He jumped back as the water hissed again on the stones. The heat circulated around the tent, striking first one person, and then the next and the next, each time eliciting an "Ah!" of satisfaction. The younger brothers found more stones at the inside edges of the tent, and laid them in the fire.

Shortly, as the cold wind snatched the heat from the little place, Juha, nodding and grinning, poured more water onto the hot stones.

That day a new baby — and the first sauna — both were born.

2

Chapter Two

Why Sauna?

"To the Finns, who have a fetish for temperature, life is a game of perspiration Ping Pong. They heat up, they cool down, they heat up, they cool down and so on. What secret police use to extract information from prisoners of war, the Finns call a good time."
(*Men's Health*, September 1997, article by Greg Gutfeld)

"Why sauna?" my friend Jerry asks. "Why do people do that? It sounds crazy, like some kind of torture."

It does sound strange to the those who have never had a sauna. Finnish people and sauna enthusiasts already know why they sauna. It's simple: it feels so good. People like Jerry, the author of the quote at the beginning of this chapter, Greg Gutfeld, and others who wonder about the sanity of those who appreciate saunas, will be able to appreciate the sauna after reading this book.

In the old days, as a matter of course, people in every country performed very hard physical labor. In *Sauna, The Finnish Bath*, H.J. Viherjuuri notes that, "The need for a perspiration bath has arisen in those countries where people have had to do exceptionally heavy physical work, such as clearing land by burning." Those people recognized the need to perspire rather than to wash, in order to make their muscles supple and strong before they could continue heavy work.

Over time, the sauna took on other uses. The Finnish Sauna Society in Helsinki, Finland, identifies five reasons why people of all cultures over the ages have taken sweat baths: as religious ceremonies, to heal illnesses, to cleanse the body, for relaxation, and for the social life.

Saunas were also used for house or farm chores that required heat or water because a sauna could be kept clean and bacteria-free — for birthing and preparing food.

In the past, people in Finland and North America used saunas for all of those reasons, but today the once-practical reasons of treating diseases, birthing babies, and preparing food aren't practical anymore. Nor is a religious tradition connected with most saunas today.

Deep Cleaning, No, Soothing; Deep Cleaning, No, Soothing . . .

Today the main reason saunas are chosen is for their deep-cleaning effects on the body. (See more about this in Chapter 10 on Health.)

But the sauna is more than a slow way to get clean: it soothes and provides invigorating mental regeneration.

One reason people take saunas is to relax and enjoy the solitude. Photo from Saunatec, Inc.

"Nowadays," according to the Finnish Sauna Society, "people go to sauna mainly for its relaxing effect. After a proper bath, you always feel better. It may be due to release of endorphins, although we do not know it for sure. But the mechanism is not important, [what is] important is that you really feel better. Both body and soul are cleansed in a Finnish sauna."

While it is possible to feel refreshed from a shower, or soak out tiredness in a tub bath, the sauna far surpasses either as a means of rejuvenation. Amidst the smell of steam, herbs, and soap, the sounds of water splashed on hot rocks and the licking flames of a wood fire, and the dim light of a lantern, one can ponder life, feelings, the world's great problems. In the sauna, thoughts can soar.

Sergei Khrushchev, son of Nikita and a recent citizen of the United States, who lives in Providence, Rhode Island, did just that. "I remember when I wrote one book. I went to the sauna with my notebook, where ideas came to my mind. I then included them in the book the next day, I think it's very important for you to think about many things when you're there."

In fact, great philosophical concerns are raised in the sauna, as Mike Johnson, of Maplewood, Minnesota, can attest, remembering as a youth attending summer camp at the end of the Gunflint Trail in northeastern Minnesota.

Late one night, he and friends passed time taking a sauna in a building located away from the camp, which meant a long walk back. When he was finished, he took off alone to return to camp and to bed.

He hadn't planned on staying in the sauna until after dark, so he had no flashlight. He walked slowly in the dark, feeling ahead with his hands until, some distance down the trail, he ran into a large solid object across the path. It felt like a huge tree. He was stymied, because he didn't remember a tree across the trail anywhere on the path.

Mike figured he had taken the wrong path, so he retraced his steps back to the sauna, regrouped his directions, carefully chose his path, and tried once more. Boom! Again he bumped into the same huge object blocking his way. He could not fathom how he had taken the wrong path twice in a row.

Back at the sauna, he consulted with his fellow bathers. They hooted at him. "A tree in the path? I'm sure! No way." Positive of the object, but unsure why it was there, Mike finally chose a longer way back to camp, skirting the object. Back at camp he repeated his story, and received similar disbelieving remarks.

The next morning, he went out to check. It didn't take him long to discover what had happened, and to get the last laugh: while he and his friends had been relaxing in the sauna, they had gotten so mellow that they hadn't heard a massive tree fall nearby, and for no discernible reason: no wind or storm.

Which brings up the philosophical question: if a tree falls in the forest while taking a sauna, and no one hears it, did it really fall? And did it make any sound?

This is a question best pondered and answered only in a relaxing sauna.

Mihael Cankar, an avid sauna-goer who amassed a remarkable sauna site on the Internet says, "Sauna is not just any household building or washroom, where one carries out everyday tasks. Sauna is traditionally a special place. In essence it is unassuming, quiet, calm, meditative. And that is what it expects from the bather, too. One does not go to sauna merely to wash, but also to relax and freshen up and to be revived both mentally and physically."

Is it possible to be refreshed after sweating? Beatrice Ojakangas, the well-known Minnesota cook, would concur. "Both summer and winter the sauna was stoked up. It was the most refreshing thing, even when we'd spent the day sweating in the hayfields and the weather was hot and humid."

Say "Present"

Finally, modern saunas build a sense of community. Finns commonly regard the sauna as a place to talk, tell stories and spend time with friends. Whereas Finns might shower to get clean, they go to sauna to increase the feeling of togetherness and closeness. This sense of sauna camaraderie is uncommon Americans today.

But it is important for Finns to share their gift of sauna with others. Sylvia Krampl of Graz, Austria, tells the story of how her family discovered, and rediscovered, the Finnish sauna. During World War II, her father, a nineteen-year-old Austrian was conscripted into the German army and stationed at Murmansk. There he and other young soldiers not used to the rough climate all fell sick. But the Finnish people were friendly to the young Austrians and introduced them to sauna—a way of staying warm, clean, connected to friends and rejuvenated, all at the same time.

Most of the conscripts liked the sauna because it helped them stave off cold and colds. But the soldiers couldn't leave their posts whenever they wanted to join the Finns for sauna bath, so they created their own makeshift saunas using materials at hand. The sauna helped them to survive the war. "It was a very good thing during a very bad time," remembers Krampl's father.

When the soldiers returned to Austria, they might have liked to build saunas of their own, but there was no time, no money, and no wood to spare for such a project. The young soldier told his family about saunas and encouraged them to try it. When his daughter was fourteen, she found her first opportunity. But—it was too hot, it was too strange. She was unconvinced.

Time passed again, and Sylvia visited her AFS sister, Kristin Rajala, in North Oaks, Minnesota, who promptly offered her —a sauna. After several sessions in a variety of saunas, Sylvia finally understood what her father had experienced more than fifty years earlier— rejuvenation, camaraderie, incredible cleansing.

Then she hatched a plan—to convert her perfect-sized garden shed back home into an outdoor sauna. Though she

Years after hearing her father's World War II sauna stories from Murmansk, Sylvia Krampl of Graz, Austria, discovers the pleasures of sauna for herself.

will need a special permit, because most Austrian saunas are built into cellars, she eagerly plans to offer her father one of the first steams.

And More

In short, the sauna makes you healthier. As Dr. Ilka Vuori says in "Healthy and Unhealthy Sauna Bathing," in *Annals of Clinical Research*, "Sauna means health in the sense of good hygiene, relief of aches and pains, companionship, leisure time, freedom from everyday cares, physical and mental relaxation, good sleep and thus, general well-being."

The perspiration ping-pong, as Gutfield calls it, induces all these benefits, as every new sauna-goer discovers, and every regular sauna-goer knows.

Chapter Three

The Sauna Lexicon

Avantouinti – swimming in a hole cut into lake or sea ice.

What fun is it to learn authentic traditions without knowing the authentic vocabulary? Use these words to impress non-Finn friends. However, a third-generation Finn-American who did not grow up hearing Finn spoken (like me) may encounter smothered snickering from real speakers when showing off these new words. Even so, it's fun to try. Give it a whirl while the *kiuas* heats up. (See below)

The Finnish Sauna Society offers these suggestions for pronouncing the Finnish words:

* each character (consonant or vowel) is always pronounced the same way, i.e. every Finnish word is pronounced exactly as spelled (and vice versa).

* single characters carry a short pronunciation, and double ones long.

* the pronunciation is close to Spanish or Italian, only the consonants are softer.

* the stress is always on the first syllable.

* the special dotted vowels "a" and "o" follow the above rule and sound as in German or Swedish (Get extra tutoring from native speaker).

Ta-Daa!

Sauna (sow'-na.) According to Tim Bird, in *Blue Skies*, Finnair's inflight magazine, sauna is the only Finnish word that has entered the world vocabulary. It became an official English word in the 1880s, the only Finnish word to be adopted into English.

Remember "Ow"?

The word is pronounced by Finnish people as (sow-na). This pronunciation retains its ethnic heritage, much like the German word "sauerkraut." By frequently mispromouncing the word "sauna," Americans encourage the impression of "sauna-lite." People who pronounce the German food correctly can also pronounce the Finnish style sweat bath correctly, because both words begin with the nearly identical sound — "sow." Proper enunciation is a testament to cultural precision.

Savusauna (sah'-voo sow'-nah)

This means a smoke sauna, the earliest and most original form of a sauna, still enjoyed by sauna purists. When a fire is lit in a *savusauna*, the room is heated and smoke fills the air. The smoke is not vented until the fire has completely burned out. The *savusauna* was used until chimneys came into common use in the nineteenth century.

Kiuas (ke-wus) or (cue-us) or (Q-us)

The *kiuas* is the sauna stove, or heater. While the *kiuas* can be heated with wood, gas, or electricity, traditionalists prefer the gentle heat, smells, and sounds of a wood-fired kiuas.

Löyly or (loew-lew) Oy is a diphthong; no English word rhymes or sounds like this word. Get a Finn speaker to demonstrate this one.

To make the humidity rise in the sauna, water is splashed on the stones of the stove. *Löyly* is the resulting steam that

The *kiuas* is the sauna heater, a 220-volt stove in this red-cedar Sisu sauna.

10

hisses and rises. *Löyly* is what makes the sauna different from other sweat-bathing traditions. In other Finno-Ugric languages, a word with similar spellings (leil, lul, lili) also means vapor, breath, life, soul, and spirit, which suggests that *löyly* steam had a spiritual significance.

Vihta, or *vasta*—(veh-ta) and (voss-ta)

Depending on where you live, *vihta* or *vasta* describes a whisk, a thick bundle of leafy birch twigs about sixteen or so inches long. *Vihta* is the word used in western Finland while *vasta* is used in the eastern part. A *vihta* or *vasta* is used to slap oneself to promote blood circulation and cleanse the skin and thereby boost the feel of the *löyly*.

laude refers to the wooden bench or elevated platform to sit on in the hot room, and *lauteet* means benches, since there are usually more than one.

Lauteet are placed in a series, rising high in the room, so bathers can enjoy different temperatures, cooler towards the floor, hotter close to the roof. *Lavo*, which is short for *saunalavo* is another word for bench.

Vihta (or *vasta*) made of cedar boughs hangs from the window inside the Ray Laitenen sauna.

Chapter Four

Some Like It Hot
How to Take a Sauna

"According to Finnish legends, a sauna elf, Sauntonttu, is a little old bearded guy who lives below the sauna benches. He gets very angry if the bathers don't behave themselves. If they don't, he makes the sauna less enjoyable, and in extreme cases, he will burn the sauna down and move elsewhere. You're supposed to leave some wood burning for the sauna elf, who also needs his share."
Mauri Haikola.

There are few rules for taking a sauna; it's common sense, really: stay only as long as it feels comfortable and return to the heat room as often as desired.

The basics for taking a sauna are:
      1. Heat up,
      2. Cool down (repeat as desired),
      3. Wash off.

Plan to spend lots of time, because part of the idea is to relax. How much time is enough? Anywhere from forty-five minutes to an entire afternoon (or evening) for a full "three-course sauna." The Kangas Sauna in Thunder Bay, Ontario, usually rents their sauna suites for an hour and a half. How long to spend in the sauna is personal: how one feels on a particular day, what day of the week or time of the day it is, if others are waiting, whose sauna it is and what kind

12

it is, by a lake or in the city. There is no correct amount of time needed to take a sauna.

Wait at least an hour after a big meal. Otherwise, the blood
needed to digest food will be diverted to the skin capillaries. Neither
the meal nor the sauna will be a great treat. If time is limited, take the
sauna first, enjoy the meal afterward, the "bathe now, eat later" plan,
according to enthusiast Bernhard Hillila, author of *The Sauna Is . . .*

Even though some people get thirsty just thinking about a
sauna, they should never try to replace, in advance, the entire quart
of water typically lost in an average sauna. Be wary of drinking alcohol, though. The sauna intensifies the effect of alcohol, and nobody
wants to be uncoordinated near a very hot stove. I. Vuori, in *Annals of
Clinical Research*, says, "Alcohol intake of more than a bottle or so of
beer before or during a sauna in combination with the ice-cold bath
could be called 'Finnish roulette.'"

Preparing for a sauna takes time. An electric stove heats up in
an hour, while a wood-fired stove takes longer. While the fire is heating, supplies can be gathered: towels, wash cloths, soap, shampoo,
loofah (a *vasta/vihta* for the brave), slippers, even a beverage for
between-course refreshments. Plus, clean clothes or a robe for after
the sauna. Once at the sauna, nobody will feel like returning for
something needed but forgotten.

Bathers need to decide what to wear: birthday or bathing suit.
As in taking a shower, nude is nicer. Try not to be too shy. As a guest,
ask the hosts, and do what they do. They typically will try to make
sure their guests are comfortable. There's a whole chapter on this
later.

Glass, metal, and plastic conduct heat well, so they will not be
fun in the sauna. Glasses fog up and become unusable. Mike Johnson
of Maplewood recalled that when a friend left sunglasses inside,
"They melted!" Some leave their disposable contacts in, but if a person's eyes are susceptible to dryness, contacts should be removed
also. Not being able to see is not without its own dangers, however.

Remove jewelry, especially loose earrings, watches and
bracelets—they get really hot, and heat, sweat, and steam can cause
damage. Some bathers leave rings on, but hot metal and skin both
swell, and rings may be suddenly very constricting. As a twelve-year-
old, Brenda Silkman of Waite Park, Minnesota, fell asleep in a sauna

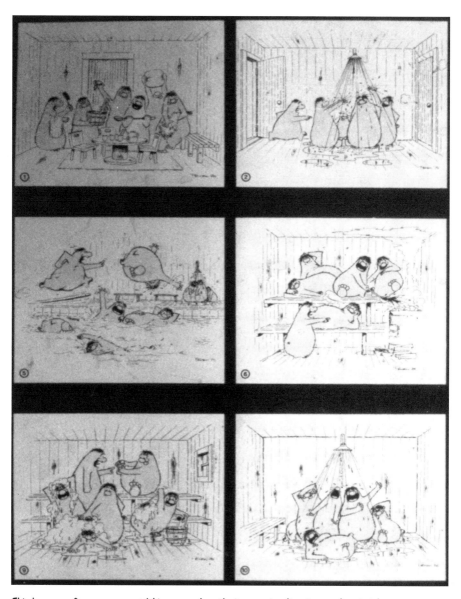

This humorous German sauna art (this page and next) gives precise directions on how to take a sauna.

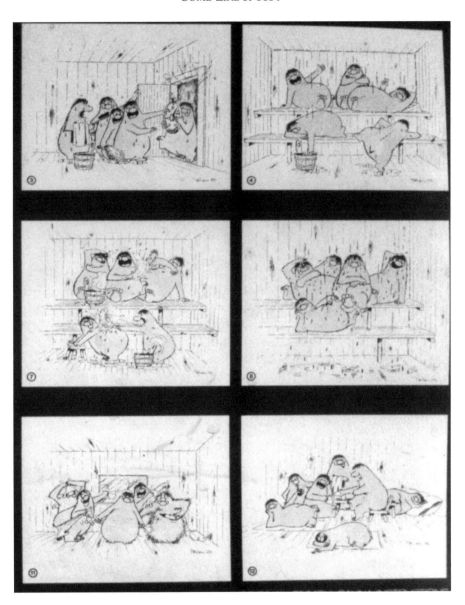

wearing a crucifix necklace and woke up to find the image burned into her skin. "That whitish scar stayed with me for a long time," she says.

Cheers!

It is tempting to bring a beverage into the sauna, but few work well because most

Though buckets and a bather reflect sauna themes, jewelry in the sauna is not recommended. Pewter pin and earrings were designed by Sheila Toye of Canada.

containers get hot very quickly. Wood works, but who has wooden beverage glasses?

If possible, shower immediately before entering the sauna. Finnish people consider it polite and hygienic. A shower rinses off perfumes, body oils, and dirt. In addition, the wetness desensitizes the skin slightly to the intense heat, alleviating anxiety about the heat.

The Finnish Sauna Society suggests bringing a towel along to sit on when entering the heat room. This makes it easier to sit on the hot benches, and it's more hygienic, especially when in the nude.

Either sitting or reclining on the benches is fine. The top bench will be hotter than a lower one, often a sixty to seventy degree difference between the head and the toes. Choose a lower bench for the first few saunas, especially if the temperature is high (194 to 212 degrees Fahrenheit or ninety to 100 degrees Centigrade). Some people spend half their time lying down, either with their feet up (look for a foot ledge) or with their heads elevated on a head rest. Relax. Let the mind float.

After a while people begin to sweat, the body's reaction to maintaining its temperature. This is not a reaction to the humid atmosphere. In the sauna,

Wood headrests and footrests enable bathers to lie down while they enjoy a sauna. The body experiences a more even temperature while lying down. Photo from Saunatec, Inc.

16

sweat ducts let loose, and the pores pour. Athletes, and others with efficient sweat systems, will sweat faster.

Hosts may "make water" for bathers. Don't worry — it's not urine, and it's not an act of God. It's how Finnish-Americans refer to preparing a bucket of the right-temperature water for the sauna. This bucket of water could be used for washing up or dipping the wash cloth or rinsing off the soapy cloth. My dad makes a foot soak with his bucket of water. Personal preference. Some pour their water over themselves during the final cool-down, too.

Sauna art provides a humorous view of the preferences of different bathers during a sauna.

When comfortable with the heat, maybe five to ten minutes into the sauna, it is time to splash a little water on the rocks — perhaps a dipperful — from a separate bucket of non-soapy water. Hot water is preferred for making the brief steam called *löyly*. (More on this later.)

Sprinkle the dipperful over all the rocks rather than dumping it just in one place. The steam that arises feels tingly. The closer a person sits to the *kiuas* (stove), the faster one feels this *löyly*. After a few seconds, it's over.

This is one of my favorite moments. First I hear the sizzle of water hitting the rocks, and then successive "Aahhs," down the line, until I feel it, and say my "Aahh." I love this litany of sounds, the steam and the reactions.

Some people feel anxious about the steam. If so, or if the hot dry air is painful, a wet wash cloth held over the nose helps a person to breathe right after someone has tossed water on the rocks and the steam really pumps up for a few seconds.

Wait several minutes for the body to adjust to steam. Relax. Before adding more water, check with others to see when they're ready. Then try another dipperful of water. Experiment a bit to see how much steam feels best.

Cool, Man (Or Woman)

After being in the sauna from five to thirty minutes, the body will be perspiring freely. Individuals will know when their limit is reached. Then it's time to leave and cool down. Many options may be open for this, depending on the season and location:

1. Sit on a bench in the dressing room, or lie down. Sit outside.
2. Take a cool shower, the cooler the better.
3. Swim in a lake. (Staying in water shallower than chest-deep is wise. Diving is actually dangerous.) Jump in a plunge tank.
4. Pour a bucket of water over oneself, cool is more refreshing.
5. Run under the sprinkler.
6. If the bather gets heated up properly, and the season permits, jump in a hole (previously cut) in the ice of a lake or roll in the snow. Choose soft, new snow—crusty icy snow is very scratchy. How long to stay in the ice water or snow is up to the individual—a dip, a few strokes, even longer. Flip-flops, socks, or other foot coverings make it easier to negotiate paths to and from the lake or where the snow is soft.

Diving head-first into cold water can be lethal, so jump in feet first or simply walk in. In frigid water, ice chunks can be a hazard. Jude Jalonen of Ely, Minnesota, remembers her brother-in-law cracked his head. So did my dad, who says that despite the bloody scrape, he went to church the next day, Easter.

18

Cooling off after a sauna is an important part of the process, whether that includes swimming (above), sitting outdoors or showering. Sauna bather ready to take the plunge (right). This sauna t-shirt was designed by the author in the late 1970s for her family.

Do all Finns take the extreme way? It is heartening to know that plunging into frigid waters is not very common. "Some do, most don't," says Mauri Haikola, of Oulu, Finland. "This is a habit that requires a healthy heart and a bit of courage, but it is practiced. Some enthusiasts think sauna in the winter is nothing without a quick swim in the snow or freezing water. Of course, others think this is sheer madness."

How does the body adjust to these 100 to 200 degree changes? Mikkel Aaland says heat escapes from the body slowly, which allows a person to stay longer outside in cold weather without feeling the cold.

Whichever method is chosen to cool off, take ten to twenty minutes to cool down, depending on how hot one has become and how much time is available, because this rapid change from super-hot to ice-cold is strenuous, even for healthy people. Let the pulse settle before such a dip or roll. People with heart problems should refrain totally from this kind of cooling off.

That describes a "one course" (or "one inning") sauna. At the end of a "one-course sauna," it is customary to wash up before drying off.

Many people, however, will reenter the sauna for inning Number Two. After the heating/cooling "inning," the skin is less sen-

19

Bathers enjoy the vigorous change of temperature from steam to snow after their sauna. Courtesy of the Minnesota Historical Society Photo Collection.

sitive to the heat. This is when many people find that they can more easily sit on the top bench and may be eager for *löyly*, or steam. This is the main time for plenty of it, for enjoying as much steam as possible.

By now the skin is soft enough to try a *vihta/vasta* (the leafy birch twigs) to stimulate circulation. Flagellate. It sounds kinky, but it's not. Cedar boughs tickle, birch and aspen leaves slap. Using a wet wash cloth and sloshing it across the shoulders or legs doesn't have the right feel and doesn't leave that fresh leaf scent. Neither does a loofah sponge or a back brush, but they're lots easier to find.

Fellow bathers may offer to scrub or whisk each other's back. It is perfectly normal to accept the invitation, and reciprocate. It feels great. At a hotel sauna in Finland or at the Finnish Sauna Society's establishment in Helsinki, a washing-lady is available to massage backs.

In the second inning, enough heat is usually achieved in five to thirty minutes. Again it's time to leave the heat room and cool off. Often dipping into a hole in the ice or rolling in the snow is easier this time. And it's possible to stay longer. It feels better too.

Combine washing up and cooling with a shower to rinse off all the dead skin and sweat, soap, or shampoo. Because the skin is so soft now, it's a great time to shave. It's important to take plenty of time to cool off. Enjoying a light cool beverage helps. Relax. Dry off. Sit.

Some people end their "two-course sauna" here. Other enthusiasts go on. I would, if no one is waiting for their turn in the sauna.

Waiter, Could I Have More *Löyly*, Please?

After washing, return to the sauna to warm up again. The sauna may be somewhat more humid now. (It may also be cooler if the door was open when everyone dashed out.) If it's a wood-burning stove, the logs may have burned way down. But if no one is taking a sauna afterwards, it's pleasant to sit in there even without as much heat and steam. Laying down gives the most even heat. Some people like to put their feet up and enjoy more *löyly*.

Come out of the sauna to cool off. If a person has been relaxing both in the sauna and while cooling off, he or she is probably very mellow by this time. To continue that feeling, take a final run through the sprinkler or dip in the lake. This might be the time to dump the bucket of water over the body, though this water may feel way too warm and needs to be cooled down, amazingly enough.

21

Lawn chairs on the dock by this lakeside sauna provide a summer cooling porch, an important feature for bathers after the heating cycle.

It's a Bird; It's a Plane . . .

Afterwards, it's time for a refresher. Studying the stars while sitting on a dock or enjoying the sunset from the sauna porch while cooling is one of life's treats. Enjoy the wonderful contentment and rejuvenation. Take at least twenty minutes, if possible, to let the body dry naturally. Sip cool beverages. Now is a good time to apply lotion or oil to the skin. Lay down. Dress only when the body is finished sweating. A loose robe feels better than regular clothes.

Before completely leaving the sauna, tidy up the place. The last user of the day should rinse the heat room benches with clean water — the head rests or foot rests, the duckboards — to prevent mold, mildew, or body odors. The wet wash cloths, towels, brushes, and loofahs should be laundered or dried. The soap should be back in the soap dish so it doesn't melt over the benches and create slippery footing for the next person. The birch switches can be simply tossed.

22

Humorous sauna rules written in Finn-speak for posting on sauna walls. Translated into English, these rules read: 1. Sit on top bench at your own risk. 2. Remember this: too much steam gets you really dizzy. You tumble down and break your bones at your own risk. 3. If sweat gets in your eyes, just blink a couple of times. 4. If you get a sliver in your backside from the bench, don't holler too loudly. Neighbors will think you're butchering a pig and will be looking for pork chops the next day. They'll be asking, "When will the head cheese be done?" 5. When you're all done or if you slip on the soap, put it back in the soap dish. Don't leave it melting on the bench. 6. If you get too hot, go jump in the lake!

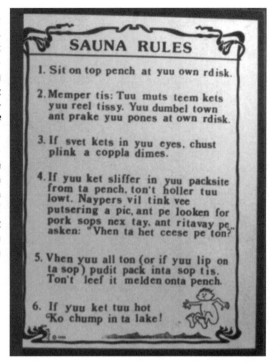

SAUNA RULES

1. Sit on top pench at yuu own rdisk.

2. Memper tis: Tuu muts teem kets yuu reel tissy. Yuu dumbel town ant prake yuu pones at own rdisk.

3. If svet kets in yuu eyes, chust plink a coppla dimes.

4. If yuu ket sliffer in yuu packsite from ta pench, ton't holler tuu lowt. Naypers vil tink vee putsering a pic, ant pe looken for pork sops nex tay, ant ritavay pe asken: "Vhen ta het ceese pe ton?"

5. Vhen yuu all ton (or if yuu lip on ta sop) pudit pack inta sop tis. Ton't leef it melden onta pench.

6. If yuu ket tuu hot Ko chump in ta lake!

And finally, *sauna-pala*—the snacks. This is the time to replenish the liquid and salt lost in the sauna. Light beverages and salty foods are especially refreshing now.

Sauna sausage, cooked in aluminum foil over the *kiuas*, is a traditional favorite in Finland. Mauri Haikola tells of being honored in his childhood by being allowed to carry the wrapped package all the way to the sauna, where his parents placed it on the hot sauna stove. The "sausage on the rocks" was quite delicious after the "sauna cocktail," a little steam on the rocks.

In The Good Ol' Days

Were saunas different when I grew up, in the olden days? Because we took our saunas in youngest-to-oldest order, kids went first. Because at least three groups waited, we heated just fine, but we shortened the cooling process. We washed up by tossing our buckets of soapy water over us in the sauna (Grandpa's sauna was in town).

23

So, we were still sticky when we dressed because there wasn't time or a place to cool down. It wasn't as pleasant as the saunas to come.

Some years later, my folks bought a house on a lake and built a sauna down by the beach. Down meant really down, a very steep hillside and zigzag to the sauna. On the beach in the summer, our sauna episodes could take an entire afternoon. We would sauna, jump in the lake and swim for quite a while before going in for another course. Sometimes, we alternated; when we left the sauna to cool down, others would reenter the sauna to heat up.

In the winter, the location required so much shoveling that we didn't use it much. Sometimes my uncle would invite us over to his sauna instead. Nobody in my family has recently cut holes in the ice or rolled in the snow, though sometimes they push the season.

Comedian Danny Kaye recorded his first sauna while it was happening. (Check out this website: <http://www.vn.fi./vn/um/finfo/english/saunajuttu.htm>) to hear how he perceived each different step—just one more person enamored with the sauna.)

Chapter Five

The Naked Truth

WHAT TO WEAR IN THE SAUNA

"Men and women use the bath promiscuously, without any concealment of dress, or being in the least influenced by any emotions of attachment."   Giuseppi Acerbi.

All the characters in Finnish literature (like the *Kalevala*) "go naked" in the sauna. Modern brochures and articles about the sauna agree. To Finns, going naked to sauna in same sex groups or in family groups is normal. They are comfortable with the nude sauna, nude dip in the lake, or the nude greeting of clothed friends and relatives who may be enjoying their barbecue in the backyard while some return to the sauna. The Finnish people are very comfortable with their bodies. Wearing anything is

Humorous sauna art of an old Finnish couple on the *laude* (bench) in traditional sauna garb—nothing.

25

assumed to be silly and unhygienic, like taking a shower in a swimsuit.

Those traveling to Finland should, therefore, be prepared. Hotel saunas may accommodate bathers with either separate days or separate locations for men and women, since bathers don't usually take coed nude saunas with strangers. But, both sexes at the student union sauna at the University in Tampere mix unclothed in common dressing rooms, common showers, common saunas and cooling terraces.

For those going to Finland on business, understand that many business negotiations are concluded with a sauna. Those on government business need to know that the Finnish Parliament has its own sauna, and members can invite guests. (In fact, for many years, weekly government cabinet meetings ended with a sauna, but this was changed when female ministers joined the staff.)

Finns may let tourists off the hook, knowing American visitors usually are not comfortable with nudity. Hosts may allow visitors to sauna alone with a significant other. Or they might offer to find a swimsuit. (Those who choose their birthday suit over a swim suit earn bonus points in Finnish eyes.)

Modesty is a universal trait, however, and casual intimacy in the company of new acquaintances, if not total strangers, is daunting. Aini Rajanen writes, in *Of Finnish Ways*, of a young American couple bathing in Finland—nude—years ago at his cousin's lakeside sauna. Their host arrived home after his guests had begun their sauna. To welcome them, his cousin flung open the sauna door and rushed in to shake hands with them. "She [the American wife] cowered in a corner, screening herself most inadequately with her hands. When he extended the courtesy to her, and since she had only two hands, it left her feeling hopelessly mortified. Completely unaware of any embarrassment, her host welcomed her sincerely. She, however, was unable to stop blushing for the rest of her visit."

Mauri Haikola, in the *Finnish Sauna*, offers a wider range of current practices. "There are no rules, only guidelines. Finns like their traditions, but [they] do not enforce them on themselves or foreigners. Usually you bathe together with your family. If you are with friends or others that aren't family members, men and women take turns to bathe separately.

"Most saunas are separate for men and women, but not all. You take your clothes off (this is not a rule, mind you; if someone wants to use a towel or bathing suit, it's not a breach of any important etiquette)."

Even in North America, the proper costume agreed upon by most aficionados is the birthday suit. Sauna buffs (no pun intended) say that wearing any garb in the sauna is like washing one's feet with socks on. Plus, sweating makes swimsuits uncomfortable. The only way to deal with this is to simply take the plunge. Chances are one person's beer gut or birthmark will find good company, and any self-consciousness is soon dispelled by the camaraderie of the visit.

Can You Say "Red?"

Naked sauna bathing is not without its embarrassing moments. Eric Grondahl of Duluth, Minnesota, remembers a few searing seconds from 1925: "Our three-miles-away neighbor had heated their *savusauna* and we went to visit them. Mother sent me to test the sauna, to see if there was any residual smoke left. She said if it didn't burn the eyes too much, I was to take a sauna.

"I proceeded to undress by poor kerosene lantern light and then walked in. I heard a squeal, and here a young lady, thirteen or fourteen years old, was up on the *lava* (bench). In the dimness I could barely view her as

Ray Doran (left) and Bob Jalonen (right) were enjoying a cool-down after the sauna and hospitably signaled the snowmobiling visitors to join them. After an impromtu buff dance, they discovered that two of the guests were female. Photo from the collection of Jude and Bob Jalonen.

she quickly headed for the drying room. It all happened in a few seconds." Fifty years later, the "young lady" returned for a visit, and remembered the incident as vividly as Grondahl did.

Donna Kallio of Duluth remembers a visit to Madden's Resort twenty years ago with a bit of chagrin. She saw people entering the sauna (wearing suits), so she walked in. In a few seconds she realized that all of the bathers were men. To make matters worse, two of them were former church pastors of hers. "I never thought I'd be taking a bath with two of my former church pastors!" She gamely continued her sauna, deciding to laugh it off rather than choosing to stay embarrassed.

When neighbors glimpse sauna bathers in the altogether, even diehard sauna bathers become resigned to the need for bathing suits. My family's sauna is located on a great wide beach near the area golf course. Out on the lake, many folks fish, water ski or troll in their pontoon boats and can clearly see our beach. Though brushy areas provide buffers between our beach and the neighbors' beaches on each side, there is always beach activity, so it's foolish to take an afternoon sauna in the nude if I don't want to be seen. Even evenings are not entirely safe. The beach is a thoroughfare, a sandy shortcut that some prefer to the mosquito-filled road.

Who's Sharing the Bench?

The grouping of people taking the sauna also makes a difference. One summer when I was in my teens, a very nice young man I liked a lot came to visit. He got the royal treatment—we spilled him from a sailboat and water skis, and gave him a three-inning sauna. Sans suit? Not hardly.

Even wearing a swimsuit can create problems. Karen Adams of St. Cloud, Minnesota, recalls a discomfiting moment from her honeymoon. She and husband, Jay, were staying at the then brand-new Radisson Hotel, and she had donned her beautiful new two-piece swimsuit to enjoy the pool area. The couple walked into the hotel's wonderfully hot sauna and sat on the top bench, she being a Finlander. "At first I was disconcerted by an older man who sat across from us, with his legs widely spread, his jewels in full view. Then I happened to look down at myself . The bra top, which had what were called "molded plastic cups," had shriveled and shrunk to a very small size. It left a waffley emaciated look across my entire top. I turned beet-red which attracted Jay's attention. I made him promise not to laugh, and to walk out in front of me. With no towel or coverup, I was totally embarrassed."

Last Resorts

In North America, then, the sauna clothes-or-no-clothes rule depends on common sense and logic, what is wisest at that particular place—a suit or towel or nothing. Campers at Salolampi, Concordia College's Finnish Language Camp, wear swimsuits as they learn the ins and outs of sauna etiquette. The sauna at YWCA Camp DuNord near Ely, Minnesota, is huge enough to fit all sizes and kinds of families. When all women and girls or all men and boys go together, bathers can choose to wear what's comfortable, suit or not.

Maplelag, a cross-country ski resort in Callaway Minnesota, has two saunas—one in which the suit is required, and one for no-suit, to ensure that everyone can enjoy a comfortable sauna experience.

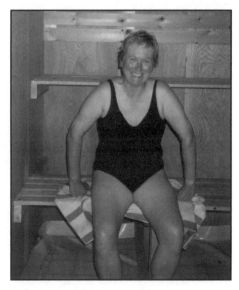

When Sylvia Krampl of Graz, Austria, visited her Minnesota friend, she panicked when first invited to a sauna. "Perhaps you can imagine how surprised I was. People in Austria are always naked when they visit the sauna," says Krampl. "I had just met Kristin's family for the first time. Now sauna? Naked? I felt very easy when I saw that you had your bathing costumes on."

Sylvia Krampl of Graz, Austria, discovers true sauna joy, greatly relieved that her hosts wore swimsuits for the occasion.

29

Sauna Queen Tells All

When I was thirteen, my father, Ben Rajala, started a Finlandia Sauna Company. For his brochure, a photographer snapped shots of the carpenter's daughter and me in the prototype sauna. I believed that few would see the brochure, and no one would recognize me, but I was naively mistaken. After the photo appeared in the newspaper, my classmates teased me with "Sauna Queen."

Though my schoolmates gossiped that I was naked in the picture that dotted the bulletin boards at school, I was not. I wore a swimsuit under the towel. Here's the proof:

Fact: I was a shy eighth grader. Fact: The photograph was taken in January in northern Minnesota in the carpenter's unheated workroom (though they tried to warm up the workroom for the photo session.) Fact: Our dads, and the photographer, wore jackets. Fact: The sauna was not heated, and the stove had no rocks. For the

Nikki Rajala and Debbie Dorr pretend this is a hot sauna, even though there are no rocks in the heater. Holding pine boughs (authentic, but unfamiliar), and keeping towels wrapped around them is difficult on a cold day. Ms. Rajala's social life suffered after this photo hit the newspaper.

brochure, rocks were airbrushed in later. Fact: If I could've worn a parka and socks, I would have. Fact: a person being photographed in a sauna may not actually be taking a sauna. Most of us would rather have more layers on when we have a camera pointed at us and clicking. Even in a sauna.

My classmates didn't understand, but Eric Grondahl, Donna Kallio, Karen Adams, and Sylvia Krampl certainly would have.

Chapter Six

Sauna Implements

"You just start swatting yourself. Spank the hell out of ya."
Eleanore Johnson of Brimson, Minnesota

Saunas are special because they allow a person to tailor the amount of humidity to personal liking, or to someone else's, if that person demands more steam. (I'm a guilty one, I confess.) In order to enjoy that *löyly*, saunas have to have water and a way to get it on the rocks. Therefore, you need buckets and a dipper.

The Buckets and the Dipper

Some saunas don't allow the use of water on their heating elements. What a loss, for many reasons!

Like many Finns, my grandpa hand-carved and banded wood buckets for his saunas, without a single nail.

The small carved bucket contains water thrown by means of the long-handled dipper onto the stones. The bucket staves are bound together with wooden hoops.

32

Dipper handles vary; this short-handled version (left) next to a *vihta* of cedar boughs has a wooden handle, which makes it easy to use.

The author's grandfather carved this sauna bucket (below) and bound it with wooden hoops. He used no nails or glue in the process. The long-handled copper dipper shows no use—its handle gets too hot.

Instead of nails or metal band, he twisted green spruce root around the pail. When it dried it tightened and gripped the bucket. His beautiful bucket is too precious to use as an everyday item. Unless it is constantly filled with water, the staves tend to dry out, shrink and crack. This is not what I want to happen to my Grandpa's handcarved bucket. However, manufacturers of new wooden buckets have solved the problem with molded plastic inserts to fit inside the wooden bucket.

Bathers now commonly use metal and plastic buckets and cover the bails with plastic hose or a towel to make them easier to handle.

Useful features of commercial dippers include a wood handle, a leather strap for hanging, even copper bowls. While lovely, a dipper with a short handle or a wrought iron one is likely to stay hanging on the wall because it will be hot to hold. Nobody likes risking their fingers to steam and hot metal.

In addition to buckets, Grandpa Ivar carved sauna dippers for his family. Wood carvers might create their own dippers, but buying them is more economical and practical.

Loofahs, Scrub Brushes, and Washcloths

In the sauna, bathers often like to remove the accumulated dead skin from their bodies. A *vihta*, or bundle of leafy twigs is the traditional tool for this, and it also helps stimulate the skin. But it's impractical to make a bundle of twigs each time the sauna is heated, so there are other choices.

A rough washcloth accomplishes much the same function, as will a bath brush, a loofah sponge, or a nylon scrubber. More important, sauna bathers can easily find them in department stores, bath stores, discount stores, and specialty stores. Stiff isn't always better, as it can also remove too much live skin from the back, especially if someone else is doing the scrubbing. Be wary of brushes with plastic bristles that do not soften.

Specialty and import stores also handle wood-handled brushes with natural bristles, but, if they are imported, expect to pay that little bit extra for their plane fare. A combination yarn cloth scrubber with a nylon thread for added abrasiveness, called the *piika*, can be found in import stores, bath stores, and other outlets that carry Finnish goods.

Bathers can try a variety of traditional and modern scrubbers, brushes, and soaps.

Some avid sauna goers even grow their own loofah sponges, especially if they have a long enough growing season for the tropical plant.

Soap

Special sauna soaps scented with birch, or infused with tar are available. Similar shampoos are as well. Regular soap works just fine, of course. If part of the sauna experience involves jumping into a lake or river while all soaped up, think of the fish and buy biodegradable. It costs more, but it's vital.

Traditional ingredients—pine tar soap in a birch soap dish next to a fresh birch *vihta*. The soap dish was created by Kristin Rajala.

Thermometers and Hygrometers

It's fun to know how hot the sauna is, and interesting to find out individual heat preferences, but knowing the temperature of the sauna is critical when children or pregnant women are bathing in order to keep the sauna from getting too hot. With a wood-fired stove, there is less control of how hot the sauna becomes; there's no real way to preset the temperature.

Investing in a thermometer is a good idea, but it's not necessary to get an expensive one. Kristin Rajala and Jerry Steinke weren't ready to buy the expensive version, so they used an outdoor thermometer instead. When they

Kristin Rajala and Jerry Steinke used a variety of thermometers in their sauna: first was the large round outdoor thermometer (the needle went around twice to register the temperature), then the barbeque thermometer mounted at lower left, and finally graduated to a real sauna thermometer at upper left.

35

got tired of extrapolating the temperature while watching the dial go around twice, they upgraded to a barbecue grill thermometer with a higher temperature range. They now own a sauna thermometer, but they still keep all three in the sauna as part of their sauna's history.

A measure of the humidity is also interesting to sauna-bathers. Not as many saunas have a device for measuring this, though. As with the temperature, frequent sauna-takers will know by body feel whether the humidity is too high (that last dipper of water forced everyone to flee) or too dry (the mucus membranes of the eyes and nose lose moisture).

Headrests and Footrests

Headrests and footrests are used to lie down in the sauna. Remember that when sitting in a sauna, the temperature can differ as much as sixty-five to seventy degrees Fahrenheit between head and toes. A headrest, like a wooden ramp, raises one's head and shoulders, preventing too much blood from flowing into the head, and a footrest, sometimes only a bar for hooking one's heels, raises the extremities to warm the toes.

A headrest in this sauna allows bathers to lie down and experience a more even temperature.

Headrests and footrests may be built in or moveable.

Clock

Skip it. This is a time to relax, not watch a clock. Often an electric heater may be set for certain amounts of time, however. Some German sauna enthusiasts use a sand timer.

Whiskers

Sauna buckets, dippers, thermometers, and hygrometers are among the variety of sauna accessories available to sauna lovers. (Photo from Saunatec, Inc.)

After the skin is thoroughly softened from one round of *löyly*, true sauna-goers use a whisk to swat themselves, either gently or briskly, from head to foot. According to the Finnish Sauna Society, "A sauna bath without a birch whisk is like food without salt."

What exactly is the procedure? Here's how to whisk: thrash, flog, whomp, smack, slap, hit, spank, whack, sweep, splash, whisk, flick — lightly or heartily as feels right.

Eleanore Johnson of Brimson, Minnesota, says "You just start swatting yourself. Spank the hell out of ya." It is not supposed to hurt, but it should make the skin tingle for a while.

On her first sauna outing, Bernice Carlson of Rock Lake, North Dakota, was initiated by the aunt of her future Finnish husband, who pelted her vigorously, perhaps more vigorously than required. Bernice passed the *vihta* test, forgave the aunt, and soon married into the family.

Why do people switch? Hugo Hellman of Brimson, Minnesota, says, "It really feels good. That's half of the sauna for me; you gotta have a switch in there, you know. It drives the heat into your body."

The switch stimulates the blood circulating near the skin. Some find it speeds up perspiration. Still others say it helps the dirt to come out of the open pores, cleaning the skin like nothing else. It feels akin to scrubbing or massaging. Plus, whisking produces a pleasant birchy aroma in the hot room.

According to Viherjuuri, allot one whisk per bather, so that everybody has their own. A good one will last for several saunas, depending on how vigorously used and how often the number of bathers "love to flail and be flailed," write Johnson and Miller.

To keep whisks from wilting, they should be taken with the bathers when they leave the sauna (for a dip in the nearby lake or other kinds of cool-downs. The whisk can also assist in washing: Add a bit of soap to warm water in a basin, whip it to a foam and apply with the wisk while flogging.

After the sauna, all fallen leaf debris should be cleaned up from the floor. The Kangas Saunas of Thunder Bay, Ontario, used to provide whisks for particular guests, but their cleaning people needed too much time to pick up the broken-off leaf bits, and they discontinued the service.

How to Make a Whisk

Traditionally, whisks are birch. However, whisks can be made of any broadleaf tree that has a fresh, delicate aroma. Eleanore Johnson remembers, "We used to cut those switches for the bath house from cedar and birch." In addition, maple, oak, eucalyptus, hazel, alder, mountain ash, and aspen have been used. Conifers, such as white cedar and pine boughs are common in northern Minnesota; even juniper is used if the branches are softened enough. Conifers have the advantage of year-round availability. Select young, tender branches with many leaves to make the slapping softer and more pleasant.

Fresh cedar bough *vihta* could be used year round while *vihtas* of leafy branches had to be dried to make sure a supply was available.

Birch whisks gathered and prepared during the late spring and early summer have supple leaves firmly attached to flexible stems. Cut ten or so leafy branches about twenty inches long (though longer or shorter also works fine). Criss-cross the branches, keeping the shiny side of the leaves out. Tie with string or twine. Made an ample supply because they are good for only a few saunas before the twigs become less supple as the summer progresses. Switching with a stiff bundle of twigs can be real punishment.

For winter saunas, whisks can be made during the summer and then dried or frozen for winter use. To dry them, hang them

Dried *vihta* (so-called in western Finland; in the east, it was called a *vasta*) made of dried leaves. Birch, alder, oak, and apen were common broadleaf trees used for *vihtas*. Alder was believed to have curative qualities.

upside down in a cool, dark room. To freeze, cut the twigs somewhat shorter so as to fit in plastic freezer bags. According to Johnson of Brimson, Minnesota, "There'd be maybe about thirty of those switches hanging in the woodshed" to be used throughout the whole year.

A stored whisk must be softened first. Place the dried whisk in warm water. Thaw frozen whisks at room temperature a few minutes before use. Once the whisk is soft, according to Viherjuuri, it should be placed on hot stones for a moment, then turned over several times. The fresh, leafy smell will permeate the sauna. However, don't thaw frozen whisks directly on hot rocks; it will deteriorate too quickly.

The sauna experience is the real joy, of course, enhanced with these sauna tools.

Chapter Seven

Spice Up Your Sauna

*The smell of herbs and birch-leaves hung in the air (of the sauna)
and the wise woman recited her spell.*

Unknown Finnish Writer

Most people like to use the sauna to relax. Others see the sauna as an opportunity: Since the *kiuas* is a kind of oven, why not cook on it? Finns often cook sausage — *saunamakkara* — on the sauna stove, says Beatrice Ojakangas. "Between stages of the sauna, [bathers] retreat to the dressing room to enjoy them, and usually serve them just with a stick or a fork — not bothering with a plate — and Finnish beer. [The beer comes in various strengths, including non-alcoholic.]"

Prepare sausages by wrapping them in foil and placing them on the rocks or suspend a ring- or U-shaped sausage from the ceiling to heat. Place foil-wrapped potatoes in the fire itself, and eggs on the top bench to eat after the "third inning."

Oil-Ay

Sometimes people prefer other scents to the predictable smoke-soap-wood. Oils added to the water to be thrown on the rocks creates *löyly* tea. A few drops of peppermint, spearmint, wintergreen or eucalyptus oil (available at local sauna and spa stores) in a cupful of water is enough to create an enticing fragrance. Be conservative, though—scents quickly can be overpowering. *Löyly* tea brewed with a few drops of beer smells like yeast bread.

The ancient Scythians tossed hemp seeds on the stones to create different scents, and the Russians sprinkled mint leaves and also splashed beer or vodka onto the rocks for special effects. Sage, basil, thyme, bay leaves, rosemary, and other fresh herbs can provide scent sensations.

Jim Perala of New York Mills, Minnesota, described the "Windsor" sauna in which a considerable amount of whiskey is tossed directly on the hot rocks. "It gets a person drunk awfully quick. How fast depends on how tight your sauna is," Perala chuckles.

Others suggest trying port or sherry, but Bernhard Hillila disagrees. "Food and drink should be enjoyed in the dressing or dining area but not in the heat room. Pouring port or sherry instead of water on the *kiuas* is a waste of good wine."

There is another caution. Alcohol, whether sipped or inhaled, in a dark room with a fiery stove is a recipe for a burn. Les Ross' friend, of Negaunee, Michigan, accidentally sat on the rocks and created for himself an indelible memory.

Chapter Eight

Buffing Up

Women are at their most beautiful one hour after the sauna.

Finnish adage

The proverb does not say the same about men.

John Virtanen

Day spas often include saunas for their customers because they feel good. Saunas also smooth the skin, loosen muscles and clean more than skin deep.

Because of the heat, blood vessels at the skin surface expand and carry a larger blood flow to the skin. This allows stiff muscles to relax and pores to rid themselves of oil, dead skin cells, cosmetics, blackheads, and acne-producing bacteria. The resulting perspiration removes lactic acid and other wastes from the blood, which in turn increases the kidneys' ability to filter out impurities.

In a June 1995 *Working Woman* article by Nancy Gagliardi, Liz Schorr, a skin-care specialist from New York, advises post-workout clients to cool down first, rinse their faces and put up their hair. "Then, take a five-minute sauna or steam bath, and end with a shower that starts out cool and ends up lukewarm. Rest for ten minutes before resuming normal activities."

For maximum skin protection, "applying body lotion after[wards] is a must," says Schorr. "If your skin is dry, apply it

42

before the sauna or steam bath as well to guard against heat's drying effects."

Because the scalp perspires in the sauna, shampoo after the sauna to cleanse away oil and dirt. In addition, special heat treatments for hair and scalp get an extra boost in the sauna. Applying heat treatment before the sauna allows the bather to rinse it out when showering later.

And, because nails are much more pliable with the heat, vapor, and water, manicures or pedicures are easy to do right after the sauna.

Bathers, both men and women, can use the sauna to look great well after the traditional one hour of the Finnish proverb.

Vicky Rozycki enjoys steam in the barrel sauna built by her husband, John.

Chapter Nine

How the Body Reacts to the Sauna

This discussion is neither a scientific physiological dissertation nor a medical monograph. It simply tries to address complex scientific information in a way lay people can understand.

What happens inside a person's body while in the sauna?

Normally, skin temperature (about 90.5 degrees Fahrenheit) is lower than the body's core temperature (98.6 degrees Fahrenheit). When someone enters a hot sauna or throws water on the rocks, their body senses the heat and tries to protect the body core temperature against the intensely hot air.

The body has two main mechanisms to control heat: dilating the blood vessels near the skin and sweating. Both occur in the sauna. Within five minutes in a heated sauna, skin temperature rises—as high as 104 degrees Fahrenheit. (Don't worry, it's safe.)

Sweat glands—more than two million of them—also get to work, trying to return the body to its optimum temperature. These eccrine glands excrete sweat to cool the skin and the blood in the skin's capillary vessels. "The skin temperature decreases slightly when evaporation starts but remains at a high level for the rest of the exposure time," says J. Leppäluoto in "Human Thermoregulation in Sauna" in *Annals of Clinical Research*. (See accompanying diagram.) So much heat is absorbed by the body that it cannot all be removed.

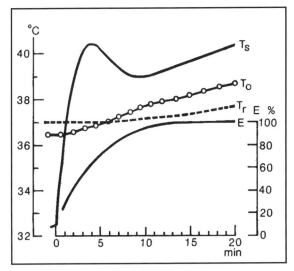

°C
40
38
36
34
32

0   5   10   15   20
min

Ts
To
Tr
E   E %
100
80
60
40
20
0

Within a short time of entering a sauna, the skin temperature rises sharply, declines when sweating begins, and builds again until one leaves the sauna to begin cooling. The inner body temperature rises to a much lesser extent. Ts=mean skin temperature. To=esophageal temperature. Tr=rectal temperature. E=sweating. The air temperature was 75 degrees Centigrade, humidity was at 16 g/kg. The sweating rate at fifteen minutes was taken at 100%

When pores pour forth, the sweat evaporates and gives up heat. The more one sweats, the more heat is lost. But, as the sauna stove continues to supply heat faster than the body can dissipate it, the core body temperature rises a few degrees.

The heart responds dramatically. The pulse rate jumps from seventy-five beats per minute to between 100 and 150 beats per minute during an average-length sauna, as it works to pump blood to the skin capillaries. "The cardiac output increases two- to three-fold to maintain sufficient blood pressure," says Dr. Lasse Viinikka, Chairman of the Finnish Sauna Society. "Considerable redistribution of cardiac output takes place: Normally the skin blood flow is five to ten percent of the cardiac output, but can increase to fifty to seventy percent in the sauna. Correspondingly, the blood flow of inner organs and muscles decreases."

According to E. Ahonen and U. Nousiainen in "The Sauna and Body Fluid Balances," in *Annals of Clinical Research*, while sweating reduces the volume of circulating blood, the position of your body affects fluid balance. If a bather is sitting, for instance, about seventy percent of the body's blood volume is below the level of the heart, and about three-fourths of that volume is in the elastic veins. "Moving from lying to [a] standing position increases the blood volume in the lower extremities by 500 ml. in average. During an equal thermal load, the decrease of plasma volume in upright position [can go as high as] seventeen percent, but in lying position only two percent." In other words, sauna tolerance is much better in the lying down position than in the sitting position.

Dr. Viinikka says the changes in blood pressure are moderate. "Most often a small decrease of systolic and diastolic blood pressure takes place. During the cooling period, especially if it happens vigorously in cold shower or by swimming in ice-cold water, blood pressure rapidly increases. The increase of cardiac load in the sauna is similar to that seen during brisk walking."

The body can lose a quart of fluid while in the sauna, depending on the individual, of course. During a normal sauna, this loss is relatively small (less than one percent of total body weight), and can easily be balanced by drinking water during or afterwards.

Other body reactions aren't so obvious. In "Haemodynamics in the Sauna" in *Sauna Studies*, Antti Eisalo compared hemodynamic, or blood-related, changes during sauna, exercise, and fever. He found that the body temperature rose during sauna and more significantly with fever but not during exercise; the heart rate increased in all three, to the greatest extent during exercise. As far as the cardiac output was concerned, it raised during fever, more so in the sauna, and the most during exercise. The blood flow during exercise went largely to muscles and secondarily to skin, while being reduced from kidneys, while in the sauna and in a fever, blood flow went to the skin. (See diagram.)

	Sauna	Physical exercise	Fever
Body temperature	⇑⇑⇑	⇔	⇑⇑⇑⇑
Heart rate	⇑⇑⇑	⇑⇑⇑⇑	⇑⇑⇑
Cardiac output	⇑⇑⇑	⇑⇑⇑⇑	⇑
Peripheral resistance	⇓	⇓	⇔
Blood pressure	⇔	syst. ⇑ diast. ⇔	⇔
Blood flow of skin	⇑⇑⇑⇑	⇑⇑⇑	⇑⇑⇑
of muscles	⇔	⇑⇑⇑⇑	⇔
of kidneys	⇔	⇓	⇑

This chart compares how the body reacts differently to sauna bathing, physical exercise, and fever. Fever raises the body temperature considerably, and the sauna somewhat less, while exercise does not change it. During exercise, the heart rate is the greatest, while sauna and fever are equal. The highest rise in cardiac output is produced by exercise, and the next highest is by the sauna. Systolic blood pressure is raised during exercise. The greatest blood flow during a sauna goes to the skin; during exercise, it goes to the muscles.

Not all bodily reactions can be predicted, and for people with health problems, it makes sense to be wary, as Chapter 11, "When Not to Sauna," indicates.

Chapter Ten

Rx: Health Benefits

"Give me [the power to create] a fever and I can cure any disease."
Hippocrates

Fever is a natural and healthy response made by the body to a variety of conditions. During illness, though most people believe a fever is the symptom of a particular disease, it is really proof that the body's healing systems are working correctly. Here's what happens, according to *Steam Therapy News*: "During a fever, the functioning of the immune system is stimulated, while the growth of bacteria and virus is forced to slow down. The production of white blood cells, the primary agents of the immune system, is increased, as is the rate of their release into the blood stream. The generation of antibodies speeds up, as does the production of interferon, an anti-viral protein that also has powerful cancer-fighting properties.

"Apart from stimulating the immune system, fever slows down the proliferation of invading organisms by creating an inhospitable environment. At 104 degrees F., for example, the growth rate of the polio virus is reduced up to 250 times; at 106 degrees, pneumococcus, a bacterium responsible for pneumonia, dies."

An "artificial fever" caused by sweat therapy in the sauna will not have the comprehensive effect of real fever, but, even so, the immune system reacts in ways similar to a disease-prompted fever.

While "just sitting there," the sauna reduces the growth of bacteria and viruses and gets rid of metabolic and waste products. (Photo from Saunatec, Inc.)

The body will produce more white blood cells, which reduces the growth of many bacteria and viruses. Longtime sauna enthusiasts use the sauna in the early stages of an illness to beat a cold or flu bug — they know from experience that the virus just doesn't have a chance against the heat.

Did You Flush?

Another powerful therapeutic effect is produced by flushing accumulated impurities from the body. The skin is often called the "third kidney." As one sweats, millions of sweat glands open up and excrete metabolic and other waste products. Sweat contains ninety-nine percent water, along with almost the same elements as urine.

Sweating allows the body to excrete urea, which, if not disposed of regularly, can cause headaches and nausea. Sweating also gets rid of lactic acid, which causes stiff muscles and contributes to general fatigue. During an average sauna, sweating can rid the body of heavy metals (like copper, lead, zinc, and mercury) which may have been absorbed in polluted environments. As much as thirty percent of bodily wastes are eliminated by perspiration, an effective detoxifier.

Other waste products are secreted through the skin. Mark Raisanen of Saunatec, Incorporated, of Cokato, Minnesota, tells of a farming couple who had not had a vacation for many years and decided to take a cruise one winter. While on board, they discovered the ship had a sauna (Finland builds many cruise ships) and decided to partake.

After they had been in the sauna for a while, they began to smell the unmistakable odor of chemicals, the same smells of the chemicals they had applied on their fields months earlier. After the wife toweled off, she realized that the smell was on her skin: the herbicides had come from within her and her husband.

Excreting sweat in a sauna cleanses the body inside and out. Heavy smokers often leave a yellow residue on the towels after a steam bath or a body wrap. Reino Tarkianinen, President of Finlandia Sauna, says when their company replaces sauna benches from public baths, they often find a thick, black layer of accumulated tar from cigarette smokers underneath the benches.

Besides strengthening the immune system and purging the body of toxins, other important benefits from a sauna come from boosted circulation. Heat baths increase blood flow, which carries restorative nutrients to all parts of the body. The increased circulation delivers those vital nutrients to the skin and subcutaneous tissue, and stimulates cellular activity and growth. "Sweat emulsifies the fat of the sebaceous glands far more effectively than water and clears them of sebum and the bacterial flora they usually contain," says Dr. J. Perasaol of the Finnish Student Health Service in Helsinki, as reported in *Steam Therapy News*. This allows the impurities in the fat to be cleared from the body. Once the impurities are gone, skin becomes soft and glowing.

For both menstruating and menopausal women, the sauna can ease uncomfortable symptoms. Sweating allows menstruating women to eliminate the excess water caused by salt retention, and it can purge the toxic accumulations of menopausal women, who no longer have the usual monthly outlet. Plus, the heat can release muscle tension and ease cramping.

Steam Therapy News also notes systematic changes in the blood's neurotransmitter and peptide concentration during a sauna, which may account for the long-lasting, comfortable, peaceful feeling bathers report after sauna.

While sitting (or lying) relaxing on the sauna bench, the body is hard at work. The heat opens clogged respiratory passages, giving relief from colds and other minor respiratory problems.

So enjoy that sauna—it's not just for relaxing. It can also help relieve poor circulation, remove toxins, assist in warding off colds and flu, ease congestion in the sinuses, comfort tension headaches or backaches and also help a person sleep more soundly.

"Not bad for just sitting there," Raisanan says.

Chapter Eleven

When Not to Sauna

Author's Warning: This information is not meant to take the place of a physician's advice for one's own individual needs. People with specific diseases or problems can do extensive Internet searches of medical literature. Because of the complexity of the articles, readers should ask their physicians to help them interpret the scientific information when in doubt.

Is there ever a time when someone shouldn't partake in such a wonderful experience as a sauna? Well, yes, there are a few such times. They depend either on what a person might have been doing in the last few hours or what particular medical conditions a person might have.

The sauna, a kind of "artificial fever," raises the body temperature, and the body adapts in multiple ways: the heat causes the capillaries in the skin to dilate, the pulse to quicken, and the blood pressure to lower. Almost every medical concern about the sauna is related to how this "fever" affects your body.

The Sauna and Eating

Wait an hour after eating a large meal. Eating diverts the blood in the system to the stomach and intestines for digesting food. In the sauna, skin capillaries open up and draw blood to the skin, which

51

means less blood for the stomach. Digestion occurs more slowly. This can make a person feel lightheaded or as if there's a brick in the stomach, or both. What a waste of a great meal and a relaxing sauna. So it is wise to plan ahead and put some space between eating and a sauna.

The Sauna and Heavy Physical Work

After doing extremely heavy physical work or performing a demanding workout at the gym, take five or more minutes to let the body cool down first. Relax, even lie down, to allow your heart rate to return to normal. Simply put: your body needs recovery time before a sweat bath, which will create physiological changes similar to the heavy work of the workout. If extensive fluid has been lost to sweating already, rehydrate before the sauna.

The Sauna and Prescription Medicines

If one takes prescription medications for heart and blood pressure, be aware that each one alters the way the body reacts to the sauna-produced stresses of increased heart rate, blood flow, blood pressure, and blood chemistry. Different medicines affect the body's ability to compensate to these stresses.

Dr. Mary Rajala of Green Bay, Wisconsin, provides further insight. "There are a lot of different classes of blood pressure medicines and each class works a different way, altering to some degree the body's mechanisms to react to extremes of heat. And a sauna is an artificial fever. Different medications take away your ability to compensate in certain ways. Your body is less able to adapt to the heat."

The Sauna and Alcohol

The same holds true for other drugs, as well as alcohol; they strengthen the effects of a sauna, and they alter body chemistry and the ability to understand and react to a potentially dangerous situation. According to I. Vuori in "Healthy and Unhealthy Sauna

Bathing" in *Annals of Clinical Research,* alcohol increases the risk of sudden cardio- and cerebro-vascular complications as well as cardiac arrythmias. In addition, alcohol decreases judgement, balance, neuro-muscular coordination, and the ability to swim.

A few beers before a sauna is *not* recommended. If guests have been partying, they should wait on the cooling bench and enjoy the sunset instead of taking the sauna. Save the cocktails until afterwards.

The Sauna and Children

A low stool was included in this sauna so young children could bathe comfortably at the lower temperatures nearer the floor.

When adults bring children into a sauna, they must use common sense and be cautious. Some hotel saunas prohibit children under the age of sixteen. Children don't sweat well because their sweat glands aren't mature, because they have a high ratio of body surface area to body mass, and because they have only a thin fat layer as insulation. They won't tolerate heat stress as adults do, according to Dr. Rajala.

"Neither of our kids (seven and eleven) enjoy our sauna that much," she says. "They don't enjoy it aesthetically, don't like steam, and don't like to sit on the top bench. Sauna is a learned appreciation."

Still kids can successfully take saunas, and they do in Finland. According to Lasse Viinikka, M.D., and chairman of the Finnish Sauna Society, "Twelve percent of Finnish children have their first sauna before the age of one month, seventy percent before the age of one year and ninety-five percent before the age of two years. But they are carefully taught how to take a sauna."

Dr. Viinikka suggests: "Children's bathing must take place on a totally voluntary basis. Thermal stress should be limited according to the age (ten minutes at seventy degrees Centigrade is too much for many children at two to five years) and the child must be old enough to express discomfort in a way understandable to parents."

The Sauna and Pregnancy

A local sauna allows a pregnant woman to participate only with permission from her doctor. Dr. Rajala explains the reasoning. During the first trimester of pregnancy, the body is developing the baby's organs. Creating high temperatures (with the "artificial fever" of a sauna) will have serious consequences in utero at that time. Pregnancy induces additional stress on a woman's heart, with circulating blood volume, respiratory rate, and heart rate already higher. A pregnant woman's system can be seriously overloaded in a hot sauna.

After the first trimester, a short sauna or one at a lower temperature, and in moderation, is suggested by Dr. Rajala. "When I was pregnant, I took short saunas of five minutes. A lot of times I didn't feel like taking a sauna." And it's not recommended for someone who's not already accustomed to saunas.

Women experiencing toxemia or having complicated pregnancies should consult with their physician before taking a sauna.

In Finland, where women are highly acclimated to saunas, pregnant women take regular sauna baths, but at temperatures of around seventy degrees Centigrade (158 degrees Fahrenheit).

The Sauna and Medical Conditions

The Finnish Sauna Society identifies various diseases, such as heart disease, high blood pressure, asthma, or skin disease as serious health risks for sauna-goers. Further, the society says such people should "pay special attention to the way they bathe. However, for most people in these groups moderate sauna bathing presents no health risk." "Moderate" here means keeping the temperature under ninety degrees Centigrade (194 degrees Fahrenheit) and avoiding any rapid changes from hot to cold or vice versa. This caveat is for Finns, who are accustomed to saunas.

Dr. Rajala says, "In a sauna the heart rate goes up. A high heart rate makes your heart consume a lot of oxygen and work a lot harder. If you put somebody with heart disease in a sauna and their heart speeds up, it won't be good for them. Certain kinds of heart medications slow the heart down so that it can't speed up. People who take medications that control heart rate might not react to the heat as well. You need to know how that person's medication might react.

"If that person has underlying heart disease, the physician would need to know how significant the disease is, and if the person is acclimated to sauna. So check with your physician, particularly if you're taking a new medication or if you're not accustomed to taking saunas. The medications may interfere with your body's mechanisms to get rid of excess heat."

A rule of thumb to assess an individual's situation: does the level of disease cause functional disturbances at rest or with light physical exercise? If it does, the sauna is not recommended. When symptom-free, a person may try the sauna but use a gradual cooling process and skip the frigid water.

In addition to heart disease and high and low blood pressure, Dr. Viinikka identifies people who are running a fever or those with inflammatory diseases or injuries as those who should avoid the sauna completely. He states, "Anybody with a contagious disease should bathe only in his own sauna." People with inflammation in muscles, joints, or the back should not use the sauna while they experience ache, swelling, redness, or tenderness because heat at this stage will increase the swelling and symptoms.

Because of the hot dry air of the sauna, bathing is not recommended for patients with pneumonia, acute respiratory diseases, and acute inflammation of the eyes or nasal passages. Those with sutured or open wounds or chronic nose bleeding should also avoid saunas, as the greater heart rate will increase the amount of blood to their injury. Those who fatigue easily should consult their medical practitioner before going into a sauna.

"Diabetic patients can take sauna without harms or risks," suggests Vuori. "However, subcutaneously injected insulin is absorbed faster than usual in the sauna. The risk of hypoglycemia can be prevented by decreasing the insulin dose or by having a snack before taking a sauna.

"Asthmatic patients and those with obstructive lung diseases find sauna beneficial because the airways are slightly dilated and mucus expectoration may increase. Sauna is not advisable during the acute phase of respiratory infection and during the first days of convalescence afterwards because the condition usually gets worse. Patients with convulsive disorders can take a moderate sauna safely if the condition is well-controlled by medication. For those with renal insufficiency, the sauna offers theoretical benefits by increasing the excretion of fluid and waste products."

Bathers should first discuss medical conditions with their physician. If allowed to sauna, the bathers should carefully listen to their bodies and exercise great care.

The Sauna Warning System

The body has its own sauna warning system: dizziness, nausea, headache, or shortness of breath—if these symptoms appear, the bather should leave the sauna and cool off. The sauna can be tried again another day but with a lower temperature and shorter time. Usually the symptoms have an easy explanation: maybe the person is unaccustomed to saunas. Maybe there are chemical interactions between the body, medications, and the heat. If symptoms persist, the cause needs to be identified before partaking of the full heat.

A highly exaggerated heartbeat, breathing difficulties, or pain point to an abnormality. These dangerous symptoms warn of heat stress or heat stroke: lightheadedness, weakness, fatigue, a sudden great thirst, cessation of sweating or an excessively high fever.

Despite these caveats, the sauna is a great place to relax, have fun, cleanse and steam away cares.

Chapter Twelve

The Sauna and Athletes
THE COMPETITIVE EDGE

"After a long run cross-country on skis, when the muscles feel completely worn out and aching, all symptoms of exhaustion disappear on the sauna platform. It is only there that one manages to recollect all that happened in the competition."
(Anonymous Finnish athlete, Viherjuuri).

Paavo Nurmi, the famous Finnish Olympic distance runner, believed, like the athlete in the quote above, that the sauna could not be too highly recommended after a race as a remedy for stiff and sore limbs. In fact, a survey of top Finnish athletes, described by Dr. Ilkka Vuori in "Use of the Sauna by Finnish Athletes" in *Sauna Studies*, showed that eighty percent use the sauna after competitions to relax and refresh themselves, to prevent muscle soreness and to speed recovery. In addition, boxers, wrestlers, and weight lifters used the sauna before a competition to help reach a desired weight.

Sauna significantly accelerates recovery from fatigue, says S. Rehunen in "The Sauna and Sports" in *Annals of Clinical Research,* "All over the world, instruction books on athletic training recommend sauna bathing as a method of accelerating recovery after exercise."

A session in the sauna can restore energy to those who have participated in heavy physical effort. Rueben Rajala of Sacramento, California, tells the story of a Finnish man who suggested to his workers that a sauna could rejuvenate them after a hard work on a hot summer day. "Being hot and exhausted, the last thing they wanted to do was hop into a hot sauna, but he convinced them. He told them they'd be refreshed and ready to go out dancing all night. And they found out he was right."

Dutch athletes use the sauna to relax. Dutch Sauna Society President E.J. Wijburg, in "The Sauna and Sport" also in *Sauna Studies,* says, "After a demanding training session [relaxation] is only possible when body and mind can be induced into a state of harmonious equilibrium. In any other case, complete recovery becomes impossible. . . . In the sauna, that mental equilibrium is restored."

A sauna after a workout helps to rejuvenate muscles. (Photo from Saunatec, Inc.)

When water hits the rocks, there is a momentary increase in the humidity. This "produces a sharper, more intense heat, a panacea for knotted muscles, stiff joints, and nerves stretched to the breaking point," says Leslie Li in the January 1990 issue of *Health.* That extra dose of steam releases the tension the body has retained.

In the intense heat, surface blood vessels expand, carrying a large flow of blood to the skin. Through this perspiration, wastes are removed from the blood, which lightens the kidneys' load in filtering out impurities. Because of this greater blood flow, which also flushes excess lactic acid built up during exercise, sore muscles and joints can recuperate more quickly.

A bather doesn't have to be a world-class athlete to get the benefits from sauna sweat. All levels of athletes use saunas after strenuous exercise to loosen the muscles after a workout. Not everyone sweats alike though. "A fit person sweats at a lower temperature and about twice as much as a sedentary one . . ." says Barbara Paulson in the July/August 1994 issue of *Health.* "Men sweat more than women; a woman's body temperature will climb a full degree higher than a man's before she begins to perspire."

But a caveat about sweating: As a person sweats in the sauna, as much as a quart of water is lost, which can weigh nearly two pounds. Take care. Up to three percent of the body's weight can be lost before one feels thirsty. In fact, a person may be in a continuous state of slight dehydration. "Since even a moderate decline in body water can lead to quickening of the resting pulse, disruption in normal heart rhythms, clumsiness, fatigue and nausea," says Richard Pearce in the February 1987 issue of *Shape*, "it's extremely important to maintain good hydration by drinking water or fruit juice before and after sweating heavily."

Athletes also burn calories in the sauna, according to Pearce. "The energy that it takes to evaporate body sweat is derived from the conversion of fat and carbohydrates in a process that burns up calories." To determine how many calories might be burned, Pearce cites Army flight surgeon Dr. Ward Dean's study of sweat and energy con-

In the steam room on the left, the water vapor conveys the heat instead of the air. Though the steam room seems hotter, it's not. A steam room is actually 120 degrees F. while a sauna (on the right) is 170 to 180 degrees F. This modular, or pre-fab, sauna from Saunatec, Inc., can be modified to fit space needs. (Photo from Saunatec, Inc.)

sumption: "A moderately conditioned person can easily sweat off 500 grams [approximately seventeen fluid ounces] in a sauna in a single session, consuming nearly 300 calories in the process," equivalent to a several-mile run.

Finally, a session in the sauna conditions the heart, especially when the hot/cold cycle is repeated several times. Every time there's a rapid change in temperature, from hot to cool to hot, says Pearce, the "heart rate increases by sixty percent or more—as much as with moderate exercise. The accelerated activity of the heart muscle increases oxygen demand and along with it the conversion of still more calories to energy."

What about the Hot Tub or the Steam Room?

Athletes recognize that a hot tub comforts their tired muscles after a workout, but they may not know that many experts believe that hot tubs aren't necessarily healthy. For one thing, "Getting into a hot tub can wash away the moisture your skin needs to keep healthy," says Liz Schorr, skin care specialist in New York in a June 1985 article of *Working Woman*. That can be remedied with moisturizer.

What can't be so easily remedied is an unclean hot tub. If it isn't correctly maintained, it can help spread such contagions as skin bacteria, herpes viruses, and even a mild form of Legionnaire's Disease says Pearce, citing information from the *Journal of the American Medical Association*.

Some athletes prefer a steam room to a sauna. (Photo from Saunatec, Inc.)

Ancient Turkish people realized that bathing water in tubs could quickly become a stew of filth, so at Turkish *hammam* baths, bathing in tubs or still waters was forbidden. The French at the time of Louis XV used two baths, one for washing and one for rinsing, according to Bernhard Hillila. We use the same principle in dish-washing—separate basins for washing and rinsing our dishes—but not for our bodies.

Some of our grandparents understood what the ancients did. Mary Wade of Kenosha, Wisconsin, recalls life at her Grandmother's house in Red Granite, Wisconsin. "My mom could never take a bath. She took a sauna every Saturday night but not a bath because baths were bad. Grandma believed that because you were sitting and wash-ing in the same hot dirty water. Now they realize that you're not sup-posed to sit in water. You have to give the woman credit. We'd stand in a big tub in the kitchen and grandma [would] pour water over you, but we could not sit down in it. That was a no-no."

And Effie DeKeyser of Gladstone, Michigan, would add one more thing. She had never taken a tub bath until she moved to take a teaching position in Marquette, Michigan, when she was in her early twenties. "How I missed that sauna! I didn't feel really clean until several years later, when I gradually adjusted to a tub."

Either a sauna or steam bath are better for athletes than a hot tub and just as relaxing after an intense workout. Both mellow stressed muscles.

Differences between the Sauna and the Steam Bath

The sauna and the steam bath are quite different, though they might seem very similar. People with very dry skin or those who don't like dry air may prefer a soothing steam bath, which warms the body quickly, then maintains that heat to soothe sore muscles.

In the steam room, water vapor conveys the heat instead of the air. While the steam bath seems hotter than a sauna, it's not; in actual temperatures, a steam room is usually about 120 degrees F., while a sauna is usually between 170 and 180 degrees F. The steam room feels hotter because the air is saturated with moisture, and the body has a more difficult time ridding itself of heat because it can't easily sweat to cool itself. Thus body heat rises faster.

A sauna, on the other hand, doesn't feel as hot because body heat is more efficiently diffused in the hot dry air. It's easier to sweat, and when sweat evaporates, it cools the skin.

In addition to cooling the body, sweating helps condition the skin and get rid of accumulated toxins. A steam room, which is hot and moisture laden, doesn't provide that benefit for the simple reason that it doesn't allow the body to sweat very much. The sauna allows the body to sweat more, which helps reduce the body's burden of toxins like nickel, mercury, and lead picked up from the environment.

Though athletes prefer different types of bathing areas, the evidence in favor of the sauna is overwhelming; perhaps a future book will be able to say, "High schools, colleges, and professional sports teams routinely have saunas simply because they are the best post-workout tools available."

Four Times the Sauna Can't Help Athletes

The sauna is well-known for helping people feel better, relax, cure certain diseases, and the like. But there are times when the sauna shouldn't be used, and in particular, by athletes.

In "The Sauna and Sports," in *Annals of Clinical Research*, S. Rehunen summarizes uses of the sauna for athletes. "In the sauna, an athlete cleanses his body, refreshes his mind, recovers more rapidly, and relaxes."

But then Rehunen enumerates four ineffective uses of the sauna for athletes.

1. Treatment of sports injuries—He advocates compression, cold, and elevation at first. Says Rehunen, "Massage, all forms of thermotherapy and movement are prohibited during the first one or two days after injury. Heat-producing physical therapy [in a sauna] may not be started before the third day after an injury."

2. Part of warm-up exercises—Though few studies exist regarding the use of the sauna, Rehunen says, "active warm-up is more effective than a twenty-minute sauna bath prior to running a race." *Muscle and Fitness* agrees: "While warmth applied to the outside of the body warms the skin and parts of the muscles close to the skin's surface, it doesn't effectively warm the muscles, particularly the deep-seated muscles and tendons." A warmer skin temperature does not mean the muscles are ready for intense activity.

3. Improvement of adaptation to heat—Some athletes hope that saunas help them adapt faster to compete in hot climates, when they can't arrive in the hot country to acclimate for ten days before the competition. Unfortunately, according to Rehunen, "Sauna bathing does not actually promote adaptation, but only subjective tolerance."

4. Rapid weight reduction—Boxers and wrestlers who occasionally compete in lower weight classifications must temporarily lose weight. This is usually accomplished by restricting fluids and foods, by active exercise, which causes perspiration, and by passive perspiration—like a sauna. While the use of a sauna doesn't affect the energy stored in muscles, Rehunen points out, "the disadvantages [of weight loss in a sauna] include dehydration, the resulting electrolyte disturbances, and a decrease in level of performance, all of which become emphasized when weight reduction reaches four to five percent of body weight. If, however, sweating in the sauna results in a loss of only one to two percent of body weight, this does not lower the performance level, at least when the duration of the performance is short."

One final note: most of the top Finnish athletes surveyed (described by Vuori at the beginning of the chapter) felt that a session in the sauna before a competition decreased their motivation or their competitive performance capacity. It may have mellowed them too much.

Chapter Thirteen

Heat and *Löyly*

Not Humidity, but the Heat

"If you can't stand the heat, stay out of the kitchen."
Harry Truman

The main job of the sauna stove, whether electric or wood-fired, is not to heat the sauna. It is to heat the rocks on top of the stove.

The rocks collect heat and radiate it to the benches, walls, and ceiling, and then the keep the sauna at a consistent temperature. If the door is left open for a bit, the air temperature may dip slightly for a short while, but the rocks will still be hot enough to continue to maintain the temperature.

That the temperature inside a sauna reaches 180 to 230 degrees Fahrenheit is frightening—especially when water boils at 212 degrees Fahrenheit. But that hot air is not boiling. Remember that those who bake can reach into an oven whose interior temperature is more than double that of a sauna, say 450 degrees, without any ill effects—for a short period of time. On the other hand, sticking a finger into the steam of a boiling teapot, though it's "only" at 212 degrees causes almost instant burns. The temperature in a sauna is not dangerous in the same way as that steam because it is usually combined with lower humidity, plus the body can rid itself of heat in a sauna but not in boiling water.

Though Americans are more familiar with temperature measured in degrees Fahrenheit, sauna thermometers from Finland use the Centigrade scale. Both are used in the sauna. Here's a handy conversion, with the more-comfortable temperatures in bold.

Fahrenheit									
149	158	**167**	**176**	**185**	**194**	203	212	221	230
Centigrade									
65	70	**75**	**80**	**85**	**90**	95	100	105	110

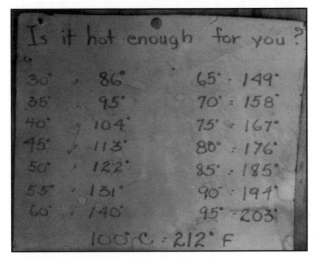

This homemade heat chart converts Centigrade temperatures (on the sauna thermometer) to the Fahrenheit temperatures more familiar to many people.

The suggested sauna temperature ranges between 170 and 190 degrees F (80 to 90 degrees C), but how hot a sauna should be is highly personal. Each person's tolerance to heat differs. Some enthusiasts favor (or say they do) highs up to 230 degrees F (110 degrees C). Though these kinds of high temperatures are achieved occasionally, they're neither typical nor recommended; when saunas are that hot, most bathers tend to leave quickly.

Other sauna-goers prefer lower temperatures of 160 to 170 degrees F (70 to 77 degrees C). The sauna experience can be modified in infinite gradations. Remember that the drier the air, the more heat a person can endure. It's not the heat, it's the humidity that makes one uncomfortable.

Saunas do not contain even temperatures from floor to ceiling, which sauna-goers soon realize. It's cooler at the floor level than at the ceiling. In general, every twelve inches raises or lowers the temperature twelve degrees F.

If the sauna thermometer is placed at head level, it registers the temperature only at that height. In reality, the temperature in the sauna is many blankets of temperatures: the temperature at the ceiling will be ten to twenty degrees hotter than at head level, while the temperature at floor level can be eighty degrees cooler.

The temperature difference — unless in a reclining position — can vary sixty degrees F.

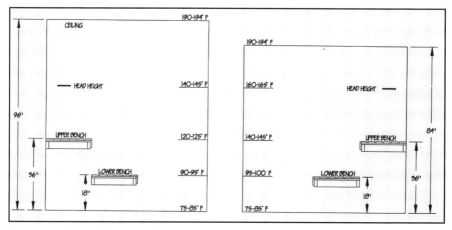

Temperatures differ widely in a typical sauna from the top to the bottom. A sitting bather will experience sixty to seventy degrees difference between head and feet, unless lying down.

One way to modify the temperature of the sauna experience is to lie down. In that position, the whole body will be stretched along one temperature blanket, so to speak, and will be about the same temperature. The heat at the toes can be intensified, while prone, by using a raised foot rest or a small wooden foot ledge. The same can be done for the head.

It's the Water!

Throwing water on the rocks is what sets the sauna apart from other heat baths. Here's where bathers match heat and humidity to their particular preferences—this is what Hillila describes as the "Finnish finesse."

Tossing water on the rocks produces *löyly*, the steam, and sets strong convection currents in motion from the *kiuas*. Whoever sits directly in line with the vapor current is the first to notice the change. (When in the sauna with several people, listen to the chorus of "ahhhs" down the bench that chart the heat current and its impact on each bather.)

The steam rises from the stove to the ceiling, and at the same time expands to fill all the "free space" in the sauna, until finally it reaches the corner opposite the stove and farthest away from it. Usually those who sit nearest the rocks, like the water-tosser, enjoy momentary steam. On the other end, the person in the farthest corner sits in the sauna "hot seat," where *löyly* pauses before it evaporates.

Tossing water on the rocks creates *loyly* (steam). All three men hold *vihta*, the leafy branches with which bathers switch or beat themselves to increase circulation. (Photo courtesy of Cokato Historical Society Collection)

In a small sauna, steam reaches most of the bathers evenly but at a slightly different time. In a large sauna, steam can be very uneven, depending on where one is sitting. Bathers at large public saunas know exactly how the heat and steam change depending on where they sit.

The airflow can be fine tuned in the sauna with a *löyly* spoiler or baffle built into the ceiling to divert *löyly* from spreading out to the opposite corner, so the person who throws the water will feel the most steam, or it can be diverted to wherever it might be best.

When water hits the *kiuas*, it evaporates, and the relative humidity increases in the sauna. Relative humidity is the percentage of water in a given amount of air, and the higher the temperature, the more water that volume of air can hold before it becomes saturated.

That's why breathing in a water-saturated atmosphere of 120 degrees F becomes difficult after five minutes, whereas five minutes in a dry, hot sauna of 190 degrees F is a breeze.

The relative humidity in a sauna starts out very low, increases as water is tossed on the rocks, drops as the moisture is absorbed into walls, benches, and ceiling, and goes up again when more water is poured on the hot rocks. When water starts condensing, the air is becoming saturated. This fluctuating but relatively low moisture content of the air in a sauna is one of its distinctive characteristic and one that makes it very comfortable even at high temperatures.

Although the humidity changes from water-toss to water-toss in a sauna, the change is usually brief, and the air in the sauna remains comparatively dry — in the modern sauna, humidity will range from five to fifteen percent before steam, and between twenty to thirty-five percent afterwards. (Remember that summer days don't get uncomfortable until the relative humidity reaches about sixty percent.)

In old *savusaunas*, the temperatures were much lower, 122 to 167 degrees F, says Mikkel Aaland in *Sweat*. Bathers used more water, and the sauna experience was much more humid than it is today. (Historical accounts, like that of Giuseppi Acerbi, describe clouds of fog within the sauna.)

The exact relative humidity in the sauna at any time depends on several factors: how much water is used, how it is spaced (a cupful every five minutes for a half hour is not the same as nearly a quart all at once), the size of the sauna, how airtight it is, how much ambi-

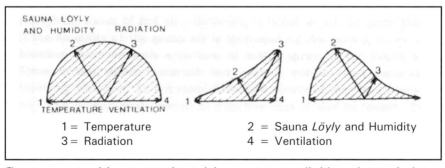

The main components of the sauna atmosphere include temperature, steam (loyly), ventilation, and radiation. The drawing on the left represents a balanced combination of the components. The center and right figures demonstrate that poorly heated stones, faulty ventilation, or incorrect radiation can spoil a good sauna.

ent moisture is in the air, whether or not buckets of water are heating on the *kiuas*.

To understand this better, we need to add information to the temperature chart regarding relative humidity. (The "Grams Water" column actually means, "Grams of water per cubic meter that air at temperatures listed below can hold.")

Grams Water	51	82	130	299	595
Fahrenheit	158	176	194	212	230
Centigrade	70	80	90	100	110

For Finns, "The recommended sauna temperature at the height of the bather's head is between eighty and 100 Centigrade and the humidity between forty and sixty g (grams) per kg (kilogram) of dry air," says J. Leppäluoto in "Human Thermoregulation in the Sauna," in *Annals of Clinical Research.* "Germans favor much lower temperatures and drier air than the Finns."

In a hot, dry sauna, people won't notice that they are sweating at first. That's because initially sweat is evaporated into the hot, dry air. When the body begins to sweat more freely, the skin becomes wet because the sweat is no longer being evaporated completely. According to Dr. Jeff Collett, physics professor at Lawrence University in Appleton, Wisconsin, "In the sauna, the air is a lot hotter than your body. So heat flows into you from the air and warms you up. But your body has to maintain its temperature. To do that, it has to remove heat by sweating and evaporating that sweat off your skin.

"How fast the heat comes onto your skin, and how fast it is removed from your skin by sweating and evaporation has to balance. Adding steam to the air changes that balance by reducing the rate at which water can evaporate from your skin. The way you can cool off is reduced, so you start retaining more heat, and you heat up faster. If you put so much steam on that the relative humidity gets saturated, or 100 percent, (at the temperature of your skin), then some of the steam will condense on your skin. Then your sweat and the steam won't evaporate, and more heat gets dumped into you, which you can't get rid of. That's when you start to feel really really hot, and feel the searing heat.

"The humidity level drops fairly quickly in the sauna, which eliminates that searing feeling. Most of the water on you comes from inside you—sweat—not from the steam in the air (or, of course, whatever you decide to dump on yourself)."

Some people believe that throwing water onto the stones raises the temperature of the room. It doesn't, though *löyly* can make it feel hotter. Only making a hotter fire (or a larger sauna stove) can raise the actual temperature.

Dr. Collett says, "You feel hotter because you slow down the rate at which your body can get rid of heat. When the relative humidity goes up, then water will evaporate less quickly off your skin, which is your body's way of regulating heat). You can't release that heat until you let the steam out of the room by opening the door, for example. Then you can start evaporating again, which cools you off."

That Finnish Sense of Humor

How much does the sauna cool off when you use cold water instead of hot water on the rocks? This is important, and the basis of a traditional trick played on countless unsuspecting newcomers to the sauna. There's even an old adage, "Dash cold water on the rocks for more satisfactory heat."

For their first sauna, Agnes Peloquin Rajala and her friend Eleanor Sjogren were given these directions: "Add hot water or cold water to the rocks. If you use hot water, you'll make the sauna hotter, but if it's already too hot, add cold water. That will cool off the sauna."

It sounded sensible to the two women, and so when the sauna started to feel too hot, they added a bit of cold water. When that didn't cool down the sauna enough to their liking, they added more cold water. And more. It became so unbearably hot (because of the increased humidity), that they had to crawl to get out of the sauna. Their "directions" were a joke, as they found out later.

According to Dr. Collett, "There's very little difference between hot water and cold water. It takes 540 calories to turn liquid water at 100 degrees Centigrade into steam at 100 degrees. If you use water at twenty degrees Centigrade, it takes about eighty calories per gram to heat it up to 100. The difference between using boiling hot water or using room temperature or cool water is only twelve percent more heat. So using hot water or cold water isn't going to make a big difference."

One little-noticed advantage of the sauna is the production of negative ions every time water splashes on the rocks. "An abundance of negative ions in the air we breathe is highly beneficial," according to Mikkel Aaland, "while a lack of ions or a higher ratio of positive to negative can cause physical harm."

"Scientists have found that if the air is charged with too few negative ions and too many positives, we become anxious, fatigued and tense," says Aaland. "This condition is known as 'pos-ion poisoning,' and often occurs as the result of weather disturbances, central air conditioning, smog, and driving too long within the confines of an automobile. Pos-ion poisoning has, in fact, been linked to heart attacks, aggravated asthma, migraine headaches, insomnia, rheumatism, arthritis, hay fever, and most allergies."

Aaland says, "Researchers learned that if the rocks were properly heated in electric stoves, the positive ions, being larger and less mobile, would ground out on the hot stones. The buying habits of the Finns, perhaps the most sophisticated of sweat bathers, has forced many Finnish electric stove companies to pay particular attention to their sauna stove design. Researchers also cited poor ventilation in modern saunas as a cause of positive ion buildup."

"It is a matter of conjecture, however, how much ions affect a bather directly during a bath," conclude E. Helamaa and E. Aïkäs, in "The Secret of Good Löyly" contained in the *Annals of Clinical Research*, "for it is customary to stay in the hot room only for short spells. Moreover, nothing is known about how ions affect the purity of the sauna air."

"The taker rules the sauna" defines the reality that the person who can stand the most heat is the one who pours on more steam and forces other bathers to move down on the benches. And when it's not hot enough, John Virtanen quotes another Finnish adage to increase the *löyly*: "Who is asleep with the dipper that we can't get water on the rocks?"

Chapter Fourteen

The Legend of the Farmer, the Devil, and the Sauna

"Soon all of Hell was afire. It was so hot that on the earth's surface, old volcanoes erupted and the polar ice cap began to melt."

This often-told Finnish legend encourages bathers to take a hotter sauna, so as to save themselves from the devil, and perhaps, a weak sauna fire:

There was once a farmer with the utmost passion for the sauna. In fact, he bathed so often that, in time, he could endure the highest heat the sauna had to offer. The hotter the sauna, the more he enjoyed it. It became known throughout the land that this farmer enjoyed more heat than any sauna could produce. Eventually, word reached the Devil himself, and he made a special trip to the surface of the earth to meet this farmer.

"I hear you like the heat of a sauna," said the Devil.

"Aye," replied the farmer, "that I do."

"Well then, let me take you to a place where it is so hot, you'll be begging me to stop it."

Excited by the Devil's promise of heat, the farmer went willingly. Upon passing through the gates of Hell, the Devil shouted to his imps to throw more wood and coal on the giant fire.

"More heat!" yelled the grinning Devil. "We have a friend here who loves the heat."

The farmer smiled and bowed to the Devil, thanking him for his generosity.

Soon, all of Hell was afire. It was so hot that on the earth's surface, old volcanoes erupted and the polar ice caps began to melt.

But the farmer simply smiled. This great heat was just wonderful for him! The Devil was not enjoying this fact at all, so he pushed his imps even harder.

"More heat!" the Devil screamed fretfully. "More heat for this dumb farmer!"

By this time, everyone in Hell had gathered around the farmer and watched him in awe. Then, glancing at the Devil, they whispered among themselves and chuckled. "More heat, more heat, more heat!" The Devil was burning with embarrassment; the Devil's Hell was Heaven for the farmer. The farmer just smiled, again thanking the Devil for such a splendid time.

Finally, in a fit of exasperation, the Devil screamed, "Out with you! I never want to see you down here again."

So, the farmer returned to his farm, sad to lose the wonderful heat of Hell, but pleased to know his fate was secure.

Word spread across the land about what he had done, and it is told to this very day to all children who want to avoid Hell and thus go to Heaven, to go to the sauna.

(*Thanks to Mikkel Aaland and* <www.sauna.org> *for this tale.*)

Chapter Fifteen

Sauna Stones
Rocks of Ages

According to legend, stones for the old Finnish kiuas *must be very special. First they must stand the test of time, rolled about and lapped upon for eons by the icy waters of the northern rivers and the North Sea, while daily and seasonal changes in temperature wreak and wreck weak rocks. Then, every thousand years, great birds wake from a millenial sleep and flock to the northern shores to find the strong rocks and sharpen their beaks upon them, rasping back and forth and back and forth until the rocks have become rounded and ready for use in the Finnish sauna.*

In Stones We Trust

Having the right stones make an immense difference in the sauna experience. Stones help to distribute heat evenly, making it feel softer and more pleasant in the stove room. Stones store heat well, so they keep the sauna at a consistent temperature. The best ones, and enough of them, produce the best *löyly*, which is, after all, what everyone is after.

But does it matter which kind and types and sizes of stones are use? Or where they are obtained? Or is a stone just a stone just a stone? That depends.

All Stones Are Not Created Equal

For wood-burning stoves, Bernhard Hillila identifies three qualities required for good sauna stones: hard enough not to crumble;

Kristin Rajala readies the wood fire in her Lake Vermilion sauna. The heater uses the traditional rounded rocks.

The new generation in electric sauna heaters uses quarried peridotite or olivine to heat the sauna. (Photo from Saunatec, Inc.)

rounded for even heating and air circulation; and without fissures, so cracks will not develop. Conventional wisdom in the Lake Superior area says stones should come from a river or lakeshore, where they have withstood heat and cold, grinding and icing.

New theory sees it differently. Each time stones are heated in the sauna creates stresses equivalent to an eon of natural weather tugs of war. Therefore, the sauna stones that will best withstand the heat are those least exposed to weather, like quarried rock and in particular, peridotite, quarried in Finland. New sauna heaters come with quarried peridotite or olivine, according to Mark Raisanen of Saunatec, Inc., of Cokato, Minnesota. These dense granular igneous rocks, quarried from places where lava never reached the earth's surface, have more surface area than round rocks. Moreover, says Raisanen, peridotite and olivine cause no mineral or rust streaks and no fumes.

Dave Peterson, of Bear Island Lake, Minnesota, takes a more eclectic approach toward sauna rocks: any rock will do, as long as it has some sort of personal meaning to him and his wife. Their *kiuas* boasts rocks from Alaska, Spain, France, Turkey, Egypt, even Antarctica, brought back from world-spanning vacations. These are rocks selected because they fit in their suitcases, without worry about their heating capacity. While the heat storage varies with their various rocks varies, they don't worry about it, and prefer instead to remember each one's origin, whether it's a stone they selected or a gift from their traveling family members.

The Stone Test

Though new sauna stoves are shipped with the best stones available from the manufacturer, some people prefer to find their own stones. It is wise to test these stones to make sure that they won't explode. It's no surprise that rocks might crack or even explode: heat of 700 to 1,500 degrees F is enough to vaporize the water, which wreaks havoc on rocks. Even cracks cause problems. Hillila suggests testing rocks by hitting them with a hammer or heating them red hot and dropping them into cold water. Stones that flunk either test ought to be thrown out.

Mikkel Aaland suggests a more rigorous process: "Thoroughly heat a sample for two hours or more. Drop it into a pail of cold water, then look for cracks. When the rock is cool, test it further by hitting it with a hammer or against another rock. If the rock cracks or makes a soft grinding sound when rubbed against another rock, discard it and find another stone. If it survives, you have a safe sauna rock. A more elaborate test can be made by your local metallurgical laboratory. It costs a few dollars."

Unsuitable stones include sedimentary rocks, or any rock which can crack, crumble, or explode under the pressure of high heat. In addition, Aaland doesn't recommend glassy rocks of high quartz or iron content. "Iron is a fast conductor of heat and when water is poured on, it becomes trapped in a shell of vapor and tends to form beads. As the beads slide off the rock a weak *löyly* is produced. Obviously, rocks that produce poisonous gases or offensive odors should not be used."

Finally, scrub the stones before the first heating. "Dirt will loosen from the stones however carefully the stones are washed," notes the Sauna Site. "This is because the *löyly* acts as a vaporized rinse, loosening even more dirt from the stones. The dirt spreads out to the ceiling with *löyly* and may spoil the new paneling. This can be avoided by placing a cheesecloth on the stones for the first *löyly* to collect the dirt particles."

How Big?

What size of stone works best in a sauna stove? Like so many other aspects of the sauna, people differ on this issue, as well. Opinions range from the size of an egg (they are probably not thinking of dinosaur eggs here), to the size of your fist, as big as a large potato, up to the size of a good head of lettuce.

Sometimes the size of the rocks will be dictated artificially; in an urban environment, for example, it might be difficult to get out and find large stones. Or, with a large sauna stove that requires lots of stones, it's easier to find a few dozen larger rocks than a few hundred smaller ones.

Similarity in the size of the stones is equally important, says the Sauna Site. No matter what the size, they will move due to "thermal expansion and constriction of metal and stones. Similar-sized stones will not block the gaps between bigger stones, and thus stop the airflow through the stove. "

Aaland cautions, "Too large or too many rocks take an unnecessary amount of time to heat. Too small or too few rocks will cause the sauna to cool after a few splashes of water. Rocks, in order to heat properly, must not be packed either too tightly or too loosely."

No, Move That One Over Here . . .

The placement of the stones on the *kiuas* also brings out different opinions. Hillila believes that the larger stones should be placed at the bottom, smaller ones on top.

Conventional placement (larger stones on the bottom and smaller stones on top) makes sense for heaters that do not need many stones. However, on a stove with many layers of stones, the smaller ones will slip into the gaps between the bigger stones, and block the air flow. Then the sauna does not warm up as fast as before and heating elements may burn out faster.

Stones Are Not Forever

Amazingly, stones used in a sauna do not last forever. They actually wear out. Check the *kiuas* for crumbling stones every two years and more often if it begins to heat more slowly. After all, says Hillila, "if they can't stand the heat, they ought to get out of the *kiuas.*"

At these periodic checks, look deeper than the top-most stones, which will look better than deeper ones. Stones next to the heating elements are heated the hottest, creating greater thermal expansion, and then minute fissures, which will eventually cause larger pieces to crack off. These pieces slip between larger stones, and suddenly the usual airflow is blocked. It's much cheaper to change the stones than to change the heating element.

After three or four years of regular use, the periodite stones will wear out. When the heating element becomes visible, it's definitely time to replace the rocks. To ensure best heating, and maintain the heater warranty, buy new ones from the manufacturer.

Part II
In the Olden Days

Chapter Sixteen

Ancient *Savusaunas*
THE WAY THEY WERE

"This was a kind of arched oven, the top of it covered with large pebbles, which were heated by means of a fire kindled beneath. The place was already becoming excessively hot."
Arthur DeCapell Brooke

The origins of the sauna are lost like smoke into a clear sky. According to the Finnish Sauna Society, "It is likely that the Finnish people have had the sauna for about two thousand years, although the oldest known documents only date back about half this time."

In the Beginning

Ancient people probably scraped a hole or pit into the side of a hill, says Pirkko Valtakari of the Finnish Sauna Society (much like the story that begins this book.) With heavy stones piled in one corner to surround the fire, the inhabitants near its radiant circle could stay warm for hours. To protect their hearth fire from being extinguished by the weather and to shelter their heads, the ancients shaped a roof overhead from whatever was at hand, from hides or thick boughs to birch bark or sod. Smoke from the burning wood filled the room and escaped through holes. This primitive structure served primarily as home. It became the first sauna as well.

Brisk rain or snow showers that invaded the structure and struck the hot stones may have provided the first steam bath, suggests ethnologist Sakari Palsi, in "The Sauna as a National Symbol," by Pekka Laaksonen. Perhaps someone discovered that the delicious sizzle from that annoying raindrop actually produced a bit of steam and the sensation of more heat. Or perhaps one noticed that snow shaken from outer garments onto the fire rocks produced steam, raised the temperature and allowed the people inside to peel off some of their outdoor layers. The concept of the heat bath had begun—with stones to hold heat and moisture to control the feeling of warmth.

Another theory offered by Laaksonen looks at the etymology (study of word origins and changes) of the word "sauna." Related to a word in the Lapp [Sami] language meaning `snowy resting hole of the willow or wood grouse," the original sauna was like a nest—a hole dug in the ground, a pile of stones in the midst, and covered with hides.

The Finnish Sauna Society, in *The Development of the Finnish Sauna*, cannot determine precise meanings of the ancient word "sauna": ". . . Its etymology is not clear, but it may have originally meant a winter dwelling of this kind."

In *Sauna Studies*, Antonin Mikolášek, M.D. in "Some Concepts on Historical Documents about the Sauna in Bohemia," identifies the same use of hot-air baths in what is now Bohemia, by quoting Ibn Dasta, a writer from the 900s A.D., "The winter is so cold in the land of the Slavs that every one of them digs a pit, resembling a cellar, which he covers with a roof . . . and covers the roof with earth. The entire family moves into this cellar. They take some stones and pieces of wood. They heat the stones until they are red, and when the stones have reached the highest temperature they pour water upon them, producing the steam which heats the room so much that they take off their clothes."

Early saunas were just holes in the ground covered with hides and rocks in the center, agrees Marvin Salo of New York Mills, Minnesota. "They lit the fire in the rocks. When it got hot they went in and had a sauna. It was the same for people in Mongolia, the Sami, the Chinese."

Smoke pouring from the cracks shows that this chimneyless *savusauna* near Cokato, Minnesota, was being readied for use. Smoke filled the sauna and leaked through cracks while the fire was actively burning. Because of the risk of carbon monoxide poisoning, bathing took place after the fire had died to ashes, and the smoke had been vented. With open fires, the entire sauna was likely to burn down. (Photo courtesy of the Cokato Historical Society Collection)

With Tools and Timber . . .

The sauna remained underground until the ancient Finns began to use tools to construct saunas out of timber. Builders improved the ground sauna with a roof "supported by beams and a hinged door, even the whole front wall could be made from logs," says the Finnish Sauna Society, and the homes and saunas rose partly above ground. As builders gained skill with timber and tools, the dugout developed into a four-cornered log hut with an earth floor. When the inhabitants recognized that heat rose to the top in this dwelling, they incorporated a shelf or platform strong enough to hold several people.

The fire ring remained unchanged, but builders later vented smoke through a hole in the ceiling or the door. Though the smoke vanished, its aroma permeated the structure and blackened the walls and benches with soot. Bathers who leaned against the unscrubbed walls smudged themselves. Benches developed a patina from the soot because they were regularly scoured.

This rectangular one-room log hut, which housed an open rock stove and a raised platform, says the Finnish Sauna Society, is the original *savusauna* (smoke sauna), unchanged through centuries.

Though common in Finland, such a steam bath was rare in other countries. Travelers from Europe visited Finland and wrote about the amazing and highly foreign bathing practice that took place in this odd structure, the sauna. It is included in *Nestor's Chronicle* of the tenth century. In the 1500s, Klaus Magnus described the places and the practices, differentiating Finnish from the lesser customs of northern Germany. In 1640, Mikael Wexionius, a Finnish professor of history, described his own country's healthy habit. An Italian traveler, Guiseppi Acerbi, tried the baths himself in 1799. His account is included in this book.

Not-so-Ancient *Savusaunas*

As Finnish settlers arrived in the United States, they had to decide which to build first — the cabin or the *savusauna*. Sometimes the *savusauna* doubled as a cabin until the real thing could be built.

Ivar Rajala homesteaded in northern Minnesota's Itasca county in 1910. He built first a cabin and then a *savusauna*, his sons Ben Rajala of Grand Rapids, Minnesota, and Sam Rajala, of Cohasset, Minnesota, remembered. They describe the sixteen-foot square *savusauna* of spruce logs, hewed inside, but left rough outside. The floor was of split white pine logs, flattened with an adze, as were the nearly four-inch-thick benches. Outside, the roof was squared, flat, hewed, and covered with birch bark overlaid with six inches of sand to keep it from curling. With that much insulation, the building easily kept the heat inside. Moss and plaster chinked the cracks in the log walls outside. Eventually Ivar added a gable roof with lumber and home-made shingles.

Kiuas from the *savusauna* at the Cokato, Minnesota, Historical Museum. The fire was built where the logs are. The stones on top were supported by an iron grate or large slab-shaped rock.

Choosing stones from his stony farm and nearby rapids in the Bigfork River, Ivar Rajala piled flat ledge rocks a yard apart on the floor to make the sides and back of a *kiuas*. With an iron rocker plate from a logging sleigh from an abandoned logging camp, he constructed a grate to hold another layer of smaller rocks, with a washtub placed on top of the grate and filled with water. His *savusauna* was ready to use. After many heatings, the floor, walls and the sitting platform became black from the constant smoke.

Many Finnish log builders used dovetail corners, says Harvey Barberg of Cokato, Minnesota. "This is a combination interlocking design and angle on the logs that does two things. It keeps the logs from coming apart, and the angle means the joints are always self-draining. You start building at the bottom, interlocking each log in. Once they're interlocked, you can't take them apart unless you start

A variety of corner construction on Finnish saunas. On the left, rounded logs are flattened where they join and finished off with a corner board. On the right, squared timbers are joined in a dovetailed construction. Note the concave-convex fitting of the logs, which allowed water to drain from the join and thus prevent rot.

from at the top and work all the way down. When it rains, the water always drains out of the joint, so it stays dry instead of rotting."

John Laakso from Fair Haven, Minnesota, remembers his family's *savusauna* in Gilbert, Minnesota, the first of five saunas in his life. The *kiuas*, fed from the outside, had to burn all day to make the sauna hot enough to produce steam for a sauna. Water was carried in and put in a tub on top of the rocks. Since there was no chimney, smoke would leak from every crack and corner while it was being heated. Shortly before bathing was to begin, the rest of the smoke was vented through a smoke hole. This also released dangerous carbon monoxide fumes that could build up during heating. Only when the fire had died down completely could people go in.

This statue of a young boy with traditional sauna buckets carved by John Storm of Bear River, Minnesota, is located on the grounds of Sisu Tori at Embarrass, Minnesota.

Howard Rudstrom, of Chisholm, Minnesota, saw a *savusauna* being heated while he visited a friend's uncle's farm in northern Finland in 1952. "They had lit a '*muusta* (black) sauna' for us. I saw smoke pouring out of the cracks and logs. That fire was going to beat the band. I was sure the sauna was burning down, so I ran out, opened the door and went inside. I felt around for a damper on the stovepipe to cut the fire down. Then I realized — there was no stovepipe." Later on, Rudstrom went back in and took a sauna. "All that smoke and heat (over time) had blackened the logs inside."

Taking a sauna in a *savusauna* was a very mellow experience, says Barberg, "but it's a one- or two-shot deal. The *kiuas* was just a pile of rocks in the corner, the smaller ones on top. They built the fire, but being there was no chimney, when it got hot enough, they opened the door, and the windows on each side. That created a cross draft and smoke just poured out the door. Usually there was enough heat for two saunas, so the men and boys went first and the women went second. That was it. By that time the stove was cooled off enough that you didn't have enough heat to make steam."

In *Sauna Studies,* Matti Kaups describes a *savusauna* in St. Louis County, Minnesota, which was built 129 feet from the farmhouse because of fear of it burning down. Because of the frequent fires, *savusaunas* were replaced on average every five years.

Over the years, *savusauna* became less practical than those with chimneys and other improvements. Eventually almost all of the old smoke-saunas disappeared, dwindling until there were only a few hundred left. But in the 1980s, the *savusauna* made a comeback, as the smoke sauna became important to the ultimate sauna purists who pursued sauna bathing as a hobby. Now there are some 5,000, mostly in Finland.

"Here in northern Finland, many camping sites, cabins along hiking routes and other far-from-everything places tend to have smoke saunas built for the enjoyment of guests from the south," says Mauri Haikola of Oulu, Finland. "If you're a Finn who likes hiking and outdoor life in general, you've probably been to a smoke sauna."

Says Rudstrom, of his smoke sauna experience, "It was different, and I had fun. I've never seen a sauna I didn't like. But you've got to be a hard-line Finlander to make [your sauna] into a smoke sauna."

A chimneyless smoke sauna. This stamp was issued in Finland in 1977 to commemorate the popularity of the *savusauna* at lakes.

Chapter Seventeen

The *Kalevala*
SAUNA AMONG THE RUNES

Annikki of fair name
secretly warmed up the sauna
with sticks broken off by the wind
evidently knocked off by Ukko.
She collected stones from a rapids,
produced dry steam
with water got from a lovely spring,
from a spongy quagmire.
The *Kalavela*, Rune 18, Magoun

The *Kalevala*, the national epic poem of Finland, collected by Elias Lonnrot between 1833 and 1840, mentions the sauna in fifteen of the fifty runes, or poems. The *Kalevala* described common sauna scenes, and thus began a tradition of using the sauna as a setting for drama, poetry, even music and television. (The poetic rhythms of the *Kalavela* are believed to be Longfellow's inspiration in his poem in "Hiawatha.")

The tradition continues today: the Conga Se Menne band of Negaunee, Michigan, plays "sauna beat" music; a popular television series "Hyvät Herrat" or ("Herrat Nauraa") is shown in Finland; and a Finnish sculptor, Aero Saarinen, produces sauna stones.

According to Mauri Haikola, "The *Kalevala* is not easy reading for a modern person, with the curious poetic structure of the language. It's made of four-phrase poems which sound very nice and kind of archaic to a modern Finnish ear. The national epic has, of course, inspired countless artistic minds, including that of Akseli Gallen-Kallela in painting and Sibelius in music."

Mythical heroes of the *Kalevala* search for an identity separate from Russia and the rest of Scandinavia and enjoy their saunas. In the *Kalevala* men are depicted bathing and talking, while women attend to the labor involved with the sauna: making the whisks, heating the sauna, making sure that a fresh shirt is available.

A future bride of Ilmarinen, one of the heroes, is taught how to prepare a sauna every evening for her new in-laws in the following section from Rune 23: lines 351 to 370, from an unknown translator:

> When the evening bath is wanted,
>   Fetch the water and the bath-whisks,
> Have the bath-whisks warm and ready,
>   Fill thou full with steam the bathroom,
> Do not take too long about it,
>   Do not loiter in the bathroom,
> Lest my father-in-law imagine,
>   You were lying on the bath-boards,
> On the bench your head reclining.
>
> When the room again you enter,
>   Then announce the bath is ready;
> O my father-in-law beloved,
>   Now the bath is fully ready,
> Water brought and likewise bath-whisks,
>   All the boards are cleanly scoured,
> Go and bathe thee at thy pleasure,
>   Wash thou there as it shall please thee,
> Standing underneath the boarding."

Aino, in Rune 4: 1-8, (Friberg translation) prepares bundles of leafy switches as bath whisks for her family:

> Then that Aino, the young maiden.
> Sister of the young Joukahainen,

> Went into the grove for broom twigs
>> Leafy sprays for sauna slappers;
> Broke a slapper for her father
>> Broke a second for her mother,
> Even gathered up a third one,
>> Ready for her red-cheeked brother.

However, she meets old Vainamoinen, who demands that she marry him. When even her mother requires her to marry, the bride chooses tragic death instead.

In Rune 45:211-228 (Magoun translation), Vainamoinen prepares the sauna and then cures the people of the unusual diseases that have been cursed upon them by Louhi, (the old witch woman from the North with teeth few and far between), by giving them a sauna-bath charm.

> He got a sauna good and hot,
>> The stones producing vapor
> Heated with pieces of clean wood,
>> With wood drifted in by the sea.
> He brought water under his cloak,
>> Carried the bath whisks warily;
> He got whisks scalding hot,
>> Softened the bushy ones.
> Then he raised honeyed vapor
>> Through the hot stones,
> The flowing flat stones.

An Internet website honors the sauna with a *Kalevala*-esque poem, complete with artwork depicting a *savusauna* and even the sound of the water hitting the rocks, creating steam.

> Steadfast old Vainamoinen
>> Produced honeyed vapour.
> Through the glowing stove stones
>> He speaks with these words:
> "Come now, God, into the sauna,
>> To the warmth, heavenly Father,

Healthfulness to bring to us,
  And the peace secure to us."

Welcome *löyly*, welcome warmth!
  Welcome healing power!
löyly into the floor and ceiling,
  löyly into the moss in walls,
löyly to the top of the platform,
  löyly onto the stones of the stove!
Drive the Evil far away,
  Far away from under my skin,
From the flesh made by God!
Come now, God, into the sauna,
  Heathfulness to bring to us,
And the peace secure to us.

The *Kalevala* is more than stories of heroes who do great, mystifying, even senseless, deeds: It tells the story of the sauna in Finnish life.

Chapter Eighteen

The Rise of "Steam Baths"

"When they have set up three pieces of wood leaning against each other, they extended around them woolen cloths; and having joined them together as closely as possible, they throw red-hot stones into a vessel in the middle of the pieces of wood and the cloths. . . . [These baths] give off such a vapor as no Grecian vapor-bath can exceed."   Herodotus, 425 B.C.

Sweat bathing is an ancient tradition enjoyed by cultures around the world. Did the Finns start it? Probably not, according to Tom Johnson and Tim Miller in *The Sauna Book*. They cite archaeological evidence from at least 6,000 years ago, which proves bathing of this kind existed in India, and later Babylon and Egypt.

John Virtanen, in *The Finnish Sauna,* quotes from the world's oldest medical book, the *Ayur Veda,* from India, which advised sweat bathing for regular health: "One who plans to bathe must first perspire. One who prepares for supper should first perspire, bathe, and be anointed and massaged." Ayur Veda relates thirteen different methods of inducing sweat as treatments for certain ailments.

"The wealthy of 200 B.C. India did not consider their mansion complete unless it included a bathhouse with a steam room," according to *Steam Therapy News*. Heat bathing clearly was an important part of Eastern culture.

In the quote opening this chapter, the Greek Herodotus depicted a Scythian custom from north of Russia's present Black Sea remarkably like a sauna. Johnson and Miller write that this practice was used for ritual purification, not simple body cleansing. Herodotus further describes the tossing of hemp seeds on the fire to inhale the fumes, similar to the Native American practice of placing cedar and sweetgrass on the stones. Perhaps the hemp seeds account for the vapors mentioned by Herodotus.

The early Greeks used elaborate cold water baths. Later the Spartans, (with whom we associate austerity and hardship), introduced warm water and then steam to the equation. Virtanen describes elaborate steam baths for Greek athletes at the time of Herodotus; eventually these steam baths became a daily routine for average Greek citizens.

Romans Go Luxurious

The Romans adopted Greek baths and improved them to legendary luxury. The grand public bath, called a *therm*, became a focus of daily social life. Bernhard Hillila describes the process in *The Sauna Is . . .* : "A complete bathing establishment used circulating hot air as well as both hot and cold water to different pools. After undressing, the bather was anointed with oil before physical exercise. Afterwards, the Roman went on to the hot-room, followed by steam and then the warm room where one was scraped by *strigils*, and finally to the cold bath."

Roman emperors supported bathing by building increasingly immense and lavish *thermae*, in addition to the smaller *balneum*, so that according to Dal Maso in *Rome of the Caesars*, ". . . at the beginning of the fourth century A.D., there were eleven public baths, [and] 926 private baths. . . . The huge quantity of water necessary to supply them was furnished by no less than fourteen aqueducts."

The Roman Baths of Caracalla reached the epitome of indulgence in 217 A.D. Dal Maso details the thirty-three-acre complex, which included gardens surrounded by a 56,000-square-foot building. The interior had a vast *frigidarium* for cold baths, a gallery above for spectators, statuary, two dressing rooms, two rooms for oiling the body before physical exercise followed by two conversation rooms. Then came an enormous hall with four warm water baths. In the center was the shower or *lavatio*. From there bathers passed to a hall fifty-five yards in diameter that contained the *caldarium* (seven pools for hot baths) and the central part, the *sudatorium* or sweating room. The sides of the building contained more rooms for physical exercises, for warm baths, sweating rooms, libraries, two gymnasiums, and a splendid mosaic floor. These monstrous baths, say Johnson and Miller, accommodated 18,000 bathers at a time.

Other Roman baths, says Hillila, also included stadiums, lecture areas, and reading rooms. Opening hours allowed women to bathe separately from dawn until noon, while men enjoyed the facilities from one P.M. until late evening. However, that depended on who was emperor at the time, as each one changed regulations according to his personal preferences. Thus, Roman bathing habits over the years are diverse and sometimes unclear.

Prostitution was banned by some emperors, rampant during other regimes. Virtanen says, "Roman law didn't have the power to intervene unless someone made a complaint. Bathhouses were sheltered havens where married as well as unmarried men or women could sell or buy pleasure without fear." The practice of bringing sex into the bathhouse, which continued well into the Middle Ages, fostered venereal diseases and problems that would stigmatize legitimate bath houses across Europe. Even today those effects are still felt.

Roman baths flourished long after the Romans themselves, but when the aqueducts were destroyed, the baths closed.

Steam Cleaned

From Rome, the tradition of heat bathing spread to Turkey, where it took on different traits. While Romans bathed using mostly dry heat, and threw no water on rocks, a Turkish bath was characterized by great humidity created by constantly adding water onto heated stones. The heating procedure, called the *hamman*, was similar to the Roman bath, but the facilities were much simpler. Instead of the emphases on exercises and sudden temperature changes, the *hammam* provided heat and quiet, and included vigorous massage. Encouraged by the Islamic laws of hygiene and purification, according to Mikkel Aaland in *Sweat*, Turkish baths became a social center particularly for women who enjoyed few other social outlets.

The Turkish bath bears striking resemblance to the large Russian *banya* (also *bania*), which uses greater variation in heat and moisture. Moreover, Aaland notes similarities between the Russian *banya* and the sauna in "ritual, folklore, and construction." He believes their development has been parallel, although no records show when each culture began sweat bathing.

The Russian *banya*, however, is well documented in ancient times, beginning with the account in *Nestor's Chronicle* of the tenth century: "I saw an oddity in the land of the Slovenes, as I here set forth. I saw wooden bathhouses, and they heat them heartily, and then they undress and are naked and sprinkle themselves with a tanning solution and take young branches and beat themselves so hard that they can hardly get out alive; and then they sprinkle themselves with cold water, and thus they revive themselves. And they do that all day — tortured by no one, they torture themselves. And they do that to bathe — not to torture themselves. And those that heard marveled of it."

All types of sweat baths exist in different areas of today's Russia. The black *bania* of the northwest is most equivalent to the Finnish *savusauna*. Bathers in a black *bania* use whisks of birch, juniper, oak, currant, or cedar twigs. Avid whiskers even settle for nettle stalks!

The white *bania* refers to the concrete baths, which can accommodate up to fifty bathers in rural areas and up to 300 in cities. "Russians are a sociable people," says P. Valtakari, "and enjoy bathing in large numbers. As many as thirty to seventy bathers can be accommodated in the washroom of a *banya*," in "The Sauna and Bathing in Different Countries," in *Annals of Clinical Research*. "The average temperature is fifty-two degrees Centigrade, and the sensation of heat is produced by pouring water repeatedly on hot stones to create a moist atmosphere." Moscow's fifty public steam baths boast five-meter-high ceilings and ovens as high as the door.

"Because of the white *bania*, the Russian bath is often thought of as a steam bath," says Aaland. Low temperatures and high water concentration create steam, while high temperatures with the same water concentration will not produce visible steam. Because white *banias* were so heavily used by urban Russians, it was nearly impossible to maintain a high temperature. As a result, steam filled the hot room. Travelers to Russia then brought back word of these "steamy" Russian baths.

In addition to the white and black *banias*, Aaland enumerates the variety of other baths found in the Russia: Roman and Islamic-type baths in the southwest, and hypocaust heating (hollow spaces or channels in the floor and walls through which heat is distributed from a furnace) as far north as Kuybyshev on the Volga River. Portable sweat baths, like those of the Native American tribes, are used by nomadic tribes of central and eastern Russia. Even in Siberia, heat baths are built using turf or clay or dug into cliffs, with only a veneer of wood. Or a person can choose to be baked in a bread oven.

A *Banya* for Sergei Khrushchev

And in Russia they enjoy smaller *banyas* similar to saunas, says Sergei Khrushchev, who built one in the basement of his Providence, Rhode Island, home. "In a sauna you sit there in the dry air, put water on the stove and use branches (whisks). It's the same in Russia, but it belongs not to only one family but to the whole community. The real difference between *banya* and sauna is size. If you make a big sauna, for twenty to fifty people, it will be a community *banya*. *Banyas* were used for cleaning before they had enough soap, like in ancient Finland."

"When I grew up we didn't go to the *banya*. I used ordinary tubs, but when I became older, I turned to the *banya*, or the sauna, for pleasure. Now I have built a typical sauna. We prefer to lie down and not sit. I think it is better, because you have the body at one temperature. Sitting is the opposite, because you have your legs at the coolest site and your head at the hottest. We try not to make it too hot. I think between eighty-five and ninety (degrees Centigrade) is the best temperature. It's not humid at the beginning, but you add water and it just evaporates. If someone thinks it's too hot, you can ventilate the air with the branches.

"We add water with some flavor to the stove, and take branches [to whisk ourselves.] Oak is my personal preference, because oak is more gentle and more strongly attached to the branches, so we lose less of them and make less mess in the sauna. My friend in Warsaw also preferred to use cedar. Maybe next year I will change to something else.

"I sit there three or four times in the dry air. We usually go in three times for heating and cooling sessions, and the fourth or fifth time use the branches. I did more with the branches in Moscow, but now we are older. We use it once a week on Saturday from November to April. In Moscow we sat in the snow, but here there's not much snow.

"The *banya* is very popular in Moscow. Each person is building his own sauna in his country house, from a big house to a very small house, but most of them want to have a sauna. They have pieces of land outside the city where they go for the weekend."

Researcher L. M. Edelsward, in *Sauna as Symbol* found a different attitude. Some Russians scorn the sauna as fully as the Finns scorn the *banya,* she says. The Russian tradition is seriously declining, and recently Moscow *banyas* have encountered competition from new Finnish saunas. When asked whether the sauna might eventually replace the *banya*, a Russian replied disdainfully, "The sauna is not even the same thing. The air is drier and it is not as good for you. We will always go to the *banya.*"

Europeans Embrace the Sauna

By the Middle Ages, citizens of many northern European countries enjoyed sweat baths. Virtanen says, "In 1679, Turkish merchants opened a Turkish bath . . . in London."

In Germany's sweat bath, called a *stuba,* Johnson and Miller say, "Water was sometimes poured on the heated stones to produce steam, and the bathers beat each other with branches. A cold plunge ended the bath." They further note that bathing was popular enough that "abstention from it was occasionally imposed as a punishment by the Church."

In Sweden and Norway, sweat bathing was equally popular. Virtanen writes that it is described in Edda-songs and other Norwegian folklore. Rich Swedish noblemen built luxurious *bastu* (saunas) into their castles.

Johnson and Miller describe *Ty Falluish*, the stone beehive-shaped sweating houses used in Ireland until the mid-nineteenth century. A foot of dirt covered unmortared stone walls. Like a *savusauna*, smoke (this time from a peat fire), collected in the sweat house. When the fire had burned out, bathers swept away ashes, vented the smoke, and crawled in to sit on stone seats for up to an hour. Afterwards, they plunged into a cold water in a stone pool separate from the sweat house.

Aztecs to Anishinabe

If the Scandinavians, not the Spaniards, had been the explorers who first observed the bathing practices of the Mayas and Aztecs, they would have recognized the *temescalli* (also *temazcalli*) as similar to the sweat baths they enjoyed. According to Joseph Bruchac in *The Native American Sweat Lodges: History and Legends,* the natives of Mexico and Guatemala used a stove-heated *temazcalli*. The Spanish missionaries who described the dry baths thought it terribly unhealthy and worked to eradicate it. Bruchac quotes Diego Duran, a Dominican friar's

This sweat lodge covered with blankets was made by George Stumps, of Squaw Point on Leech Lake, Minnesota. It shows one of the many varieties used by Native Americans. (Photo by Monroe Killy, July 1948. Courtesy of the Minnesota Historical Society Photo Collection)

description: "These bath houses are heated with fire and are like small low huts. Each one can hold ten persons in a squatting position. The entrance is very low and narrow. People enter one-by-one and on all fours." Prayers were chanted during the dry baths.

Of the native North American sweat bath, Bruchac says, "The sweat lodge is one of the most widespread traditions. Among native people, the sweat lodge is more sacrament than recreation. It is strongly associated with prayer and preparation. There are at least three major types of sweat structures: the lodge into which stones are brought in and water is poured on them; the lodge in which no water is used and the central fire is made in the lodge (which is often used as a dwelling place as well as for sweats) and the Mayan and Aztec method of using a duct to convey heat from a fire into a stone or clay sweat house."

While each tribe or culture constructed sweat lodges in diverse ways, the sweat was a special ritual cleansing, not a regular washing process. A session in the heat might be followed by a dip in a cold creek and a rest in the fresh air.

Many similarities exist between the Russian *banya*, the *savusauna*, and the Native North American sweat lodge, according to Bruchac. "They include the use of a very small structure, the lack of ventilation during sweat experience, the use of switches to strike oneself, the generation of steam by pouring water on heated stones, the use of fragrant herbs, the mixture of social, therapeutic and ritualistic purposes."

Bathers approached the *savusauna* with a reverent attitude. As the old Finnish saying goes, "In the sauna, one must conduct himself as one would in church." The cleansing of both the sweat lodge and the *savusauna* were of the mind and soul, not just of the body.

Sweat baths have stood the tests of time. For thousands of years, people across continents have heated huts to cure their ailments, clear their minds, to relax and recover, to visit with friends and to clean themselves. The sweat bath is not just Finnish.

Even so, says Pekka Laaksonen writes, "the sauna has retained its prominence while adapting itself to ongoing cultural change. . . . The Finnish stone oven sauna is seen as bringing together the best traditions of two bathing cultures, namely hot air baths and steam baths."

The sauna bath is an ideal compromise because the bather can control the humidity.

Chapter Nineteen

An Early Italian Traveler Discovers Sauna

*"The heat of the vapour rose to 50 degrees of Celsius; at first I felt
a violent oppression, and had it augmented I believe, naked as I
was, I should have made my escape from the bath; but forcing
myself to persevere, I gradually became accustomed to it, and after
some time was able to support a heat of 65 degrees."*

Giuseppi Acerbi

In an old book of travel from the late 1700s, *Traveler through
Sweden, Finland and Lapland*, Giuseppi Acerbi, says:

"Another particular that appeared very singular among the
customs of the Finns, was their baths, and manner of bathing. Almost
all the Finnish peasants have a small house built on purpose for a
bath: it consists of only one small chamber, in the innermost part of
which are placed a number of stones, which are heated by fire till they
become red. On these stones, thus heated, water is thrown, until the
company within be involved in a thick cloud of vapor. In this innermost part, the chamber is formed into two stories for the accommo-
dation of a greater number of persons within that small compass; and
it being the nature of heat and vapor to ascend, the second story is, of
course, the hottest.

"Men and women use the bath promiscuously, without any
concealment of dress, or being in the least influenced by any emotions

of attachment. If, however, a stranger open the door, and come on the bathers by surprise, the women are not a little startled at his appearance; for, besides his person, he introduces along with him, by opening the door, a great quantity of light, which discovers at once to view their situation, as well as forms. Without such an accident they remain, if not in total darkness, yet in great obscurity, as there is no other window besides a small hole, nor any light but what enters in from some chink in the roof of the house, or the crevices between the pieces of wood of which it is constructed.

"I often amused myself with surprising the bathers in this manner, and I once or twice tried to go in and join the assembly; but the heat was so excessive that I could not breathe, and in the space of a minute at most, I verily believe, must have been suffocated. I sometimes stepped in for a moment, just to leave my thermometer in some proper place, and immediately went out again, where I would remain for a quarter of an hour, or ten minutes, and then enter again, and

Guiseppi Acerbi, from the eighteenth century, illustrated his description of the sauna with this etching. Both men and women are naked, in clouds of humidity, beating themselves with birch rods, while he steps in the door at the left to check the temperature.

fetch the instrument to ascertain the degree of heat. My astonishment was so great that I could scarcely believe my senses, when I found that those people remain together, and amuse themselves for the space of half an hour, and sometimes a whole hour, in the same chamber, heated to the seventieth or seventy-fifth degree of Celsius. The thermometer, in contact with those vapors, became sometimes so hot, that I could scarcely hold it in my hands.

"The Finlanders, all the while they are in this hot bath, continue to rub themselves, and lash every part of their bodies with switches formed of twigs of the birch-tree. In ten minutes they become as red as raw flesh, and have altogether a very frightful appearance.

"In the winter season they frequently go out of the bath, naked as they are, to roll themselves in the snow, when the cold is at twenty and even thirty degrees below zero. They will sometimes come out, still naked, and converse together, or with anyone near them, in the open air. If travelers happen to pass by while the peasants of any hamlet, or little village, are in the bath, and their assistance is needed, they will leave the bath, and assist in yoking, or unyoking, and fetch provender for the horses, or in anything else without any sort of covering whatever, while the passenger sits shivering with cold, though wrapped up in a good sound wolf's skin. There is nothing more wonderful than the extremities which man is capable of enduring through the power of habit.

"The Finnish peasants pass thus instantaneously from an atmosphere of seventy degrees of heat to one of thirty degrees of cold, a transition of a hundred degrees, which is the same thing as going out of boiling into freezing water and what is more astonishing, without the least inconvenience; while other people are very sensibly affected by a variation of but five degrees, in danger of being afflicted with rheumatism by the most trifling wind that blows. Those peasants assure you that, without the hot vapor baths they could not sustain as they do, during the whole day, their various labors. By the bath, they tell you, their strength is recruited as much as by rest and sleep. The heat of the vapor mollifies to such a degree their skin, that the men can easier shave themselves with wretched razors, and without soap. Had Shakespeare known of a people who could thus have pleasure in such quick transition from excessive heat to the severest cold, his knowledge might have been increased, but his creative fancy could not have been assisted.

> *Oh! who can hold a fire in his hand, By thinking of the frosty Caucasus? . . . Or wallow naked in December snow, By thinking on fantastic summer's heat?*

Amandus Johnson noted urban modifications to this form of bathing in *The Swedish Settlement on the Delaware.*

"In Swedish towns and cities it is found under the name of *'Finsk badstu'* or *'bastu.'* These baths (of second and third class) are much used. A vaulted room (walls of brick) is heated by steam to a high temperature; to the right as you enter are a number of platforms along the side wall, arranged in tiers one above and back of the other like the floor in a theatre, on top of which lies down on a long towel with a wooden frame for a pillow or he sits upright. By moving from the platform nearest the floor to the one highest up and vice versa the heat can be somewhat regulated. In a corner is a spigot with running water, from which the bather drinks to increase the perspiration. An arrangement for a shower bath is also placed inside. When the bather has perspired sufficiently, he takes a shower bath of luke-warm water and goes into another room, where he lies down on a bench and is scrubbed and washed by *'baderskan'* (the woman employed for that purpose. It is interesting to note that a woman is always employed even in the *badstu* for men). When the bather has been scrubbed he again returns to the heated room, where he remains for a few minutes, then he takes a cold shower-bath and plunges into a cold pool for a short swim. He is then dried by *'baderskan,'* after which he withdraws to his little 'cell' for dressing. The author has seen such baths in Stockholm and even in Hedemora, a small village in central Sweden.

"On a journey through Finland I saw a bath house whose dimensions were so small that it was impossible to stand or lie straight in it, in other respects, however, being fitted out like the larger ones (except that the lower platform was wanting). The bather sat on the platform while he took his sweat bath and poured the water on the stones himself.

"Such (the author is inclined to believe) were the bath houses erected by the freemen in New Sweden. In these bath houses the set-

103

tlers with family and servants would commonly bathe every evening in the summer during harvest time and twice a week in winter. A strange scene would meet the eye of a visitor, who might happen to look into such a bath house, when it was filled with bathers, from the new-born child carried there by its mother to the old man of eighty."

Chapter Twenty

Outlawing Steam Baths
CLEANLINESS VS GODLINESS

Napoleon in a letter to Josephine after the battle of Marengo, *"Will be home in three days. Don't wash."*

Napoleon obviously preferred the "natural" Josephine. And by the 1700s, many people believed the same — that the natural odor of the body was preferred to washing. Because of today's emphasis on cleanliness, it is easy to believe that being clean has been important to all cultures, but for generations, people believed otherwise.

During Roman times, and in the Turkish tradition, people bathed as a social occasion rather than to get clean. In those cultures, bathing filled up one's day, whether a person bathed for religious reasons or for a leisure activity.

Europe embraced heat bathing over the centuries, where it mushroomed in popularity but not necessarily for its cleansing aspect. Illicit sexual activity drew as many patrons as the need to wash and restore oneself.

Cleanliness Is Next to What?

Not all church leaders of yesteryear revered cleanliness. Nor did they suggest that clean lives might be remotely connected to godliness. According to Bernhard Hillila, "St. Benedict felt that frequent bathing should not be permitted; St. Francis listed dirtiness as a sign of holiness; and St. Jerome rebuked some of his disciples for excessive cleanliness."

By the Middle Ages, European bathhouses had acquired the bad reputation of the Roman baths due to prostitution and epidemics of venereal disease. Armed with information about how syphilis spread, and using economics, religion, medicine, and any other usable excuse, civic and church leaders conspired during the fifteenth and sixteenth centuries to pressure bathhouses to close.

Leaders enacted legislation to separate the days or the places for women and men to bathe. Even husband and wife were not allowed to bathe together after an Orthodox Church edict during the reign of Ivan the Terrible, notes Hillila. Laws in some countries allowed mixing of the sexes, but not of social classes: commoners could not bathe with nobility. In other places, different races were barred from sharing a sweat bath.

Throughout Europe, however, pressure from medical, religious and economic leaders finally prevailed, and bathhouses were outlawed. Bathing became a sin for both Catholic and Protestants in Western Europe from the fifteenth to eighteenth centuries, according to Joseph Bruchac.

Once banned, bathing in Europe changed entirely; it became a habit dangerous to one's health, unsanitary, even an abomination. A queen of Aragon in Spain boasted that she had never bathed except at birth and marriage. So, it is no wonder that Napoleon requested Josephine to refrain from bathing.

What's That, Gulp, You're Wearing?

Europeans then attempted to mask their strong body odors with perfumes, not very successfully. According to Bruchac, "The oral traditions of the native peoples of the Americas and Africa mention that one could smell a European coming from some distance away."

Norway's and Sweden's communal bathing traditions faced the same pressure as Europe. According to Mikkel Aaland, "In Norway, the creation of linen underwear, easier to wash than bodies, contributed to the loss of bath house popularity."

One reason used to close the Swedish *bastu* (bathhouse) was the prodigal depletion of natural resources. When fired up frequently, bathhouses consumed far more firewood than could be replaced. Besides, the buildings either burned or rotted far too often and thus needed to be replaced, another overuse of a valuable commodity. Wasteful!

To get people to stop sweat bathing, besides the warnings from the medical community about venereal disease, propagandists added other harmful effects—such as convulsions and tumors. Swedish doctors claimed the sauna would cause the skin to shrivel, wrinkle and brown, causing frequent bathers to look like the old shriveled brown Finnish folk. They warned that eyesight could be lost from bathing in a sauna. In 1751, Pehr Adrian Gadd wrote, "frequent saunas, the time spent in smoke huts, and the bitter smell of charcoal-burning seems to be the main reason that the people of that area regularly lose their sight before their hearing."

Think of the Children!

If sauna bathers wouldn't stop their own habit, they were exhorted to think of the children. Aaland reports a 1756 pamphlet written and distributed by the Royal College of Surgeons, entitled "The Necessary Guardianship and Care of Children." The treatise described the duty of all Christian parents while lambasting the sauna: "Finland also has an insane custom whereby the mother goes to the sauna with her little child as often as every second day, which like all inanities leads to the child's early death, just as if she is wishing it on him."

Bowing to pressure in the early eighteenth century, Sweden's bath houses conformed to the standards set earlier in central Europe. Sauna use was relegated to a Christmas custom or for occasional therapeutic reasons. The Reformation made the European bath house almost extinct. Even in Finnish cities, sauna use decreased.

The Sauna Survives

But the sauna survived, mostly in the countryside. There the sauna was considered almost sacred because people believed that "In the sauna you must behave as in church." Immorality was not allowed.

It helped that Finland was less conspicuous than its Swedish and Russian neighbors. Occasional visitors, like Guiseppi Acerbi, noted with interest the outlandish and quaint bathing customs. So while sweat bathing in Europe disappeared, the Finns continued sauna bathing undisturbed in remote reaches of northern Russia, Estonia, and Finland.

Likewise, the *banya* of Russia, the *temescals* of Mexico and Guatamala and the sweat lodges of Native Americans have continued. Those traditions are respectable today, perhaps because purification of the soul was as important as cleanliness of the skin.

Chapter Twenty-One

The Versatile Sauna

JACK-OF-ALL-TRADES

"Years ago the first building to be built (on a homestead) was the sauna. It was the most important building. It was the place to be clean, the place to eat, the place to have children, the place for everything. They would do cooking in the corner with the rocks, They would sleep on the benches that were at different levels."
Marvin Salo, of New York Mills, Minnesota

The saunas of North American immigrant settlers did double, no—triple, no—multiple, duty. Not only was a sauna a bathhouse, and sometimes a place to live, on the homestead, but because it could be heated, it became the most versatile building on the property.

A Birthing Room

While the sauna was a sacred place for ancient Finns, immigrants needed something practical. They needed a clean place to use for medical reasons. Though the soot-blackened walls and benches of a *savusauna* appear dirty to modern eyes, they weren't: the soot, a form of charcoal, resisted bacteria, and the tannic acid from the smoke sterilized the surfaces. In addition, women scrubbed the benches and walls clean. Repeated heatings to high temperatures also kept the sauna sterile. Thus the sauna became the ideal medical facility of the time.

109

Many babies were born in saunas. "I had to have been born in the sauna. I was born in January and it was too damn cold to go anywhere," says Eric Grondahl, of Duluth, Minnesota. "Everybody was—me, my older brother, and my two younger sisters. There was no hospital near. Two Harbors was sixty-five miles. That'd take a few days to drive because you could only go about twenty miles a day with a horse and wagon.

"I remember my parents talking about other births. Mom told about how much handier it was to give birth in the sauna with warm water. The women wouldn't let us kids anywhere near the sauna when someone was going to give birth!"

Pentti Miller, of Brimson Minnesota, was born in a sauna too, but she jokes "I don't remember that!" Marvin Salo of New York Mills, Minnesota, recalls a neighbor who delivered all of his children—sixteen or seventeen of them—in the sauna. Longtime Finnish President Urho Kaleva Kekkonen was born in a sauna.

In Embarrass, Minnesota, midwife Hilma Rukkola delivered babies in the sauna as late as the 1920s and 1930s. Her son Raymond Rukkola remembers, "She took care of all the neighborhood women because not many doctors were around then. I think that her mother was a midwife before and had showed her how to do it." In the Brimson area, Maija (Marie) Malkki assisted the mothers in labor and delivery during the 1920s.

"If sauna, whisky, and tar do not help, the disease is fatal."
Finnish proverb

For serious medical problems, early settlers often sought relief from a sauna folk healer, who would massage muscles or draw blood, called "cupping." Cupping, says Pirkko Valtakari, former executive secretary of the Finnish Sauna Society, was a method of sucking bad blood away. And when a person is healed in a cupper's sauna, says a Finnish proverb, one will never die,

Cupping was commonplace: Jennie Laine of Brimson, Minnesota, noted, "My grandmother said everybody, all the older generation, always had that done if they weren't feeling well."

According to John Virtanen, "Those requiring cupping remained in the sauna heat long enough to promote blood circulation

The lancet (shown at left) was used for bloodletting or "cupping," one of the medicinal uses of the sauna. Bloodletting cups were made of cow's horn (at right) sealed with pig bladder. Part of the lancet shows at the right of the photo.

to the surface veins. Then this type of bloodletting could begin. The sauna's cleanliness, the sterile atmosphere, and the very hot air of the sauna enabled greater success of this treatment."

Gust Halberg was trained in massage and cupping at a school in Finland (or maybe Russia), according to his daughter, Julie Pirnat of Aurora, Minnesota. "He'd heat up the sauna, because there had to be some steam. For people who only wanted to be massaged for rheumatism, he used melted lard. Rheumatism, that's what they called it, never arthritis. Cupping was used for high blood pressure or varicose veins."

Pirnat remembers how her father would get a hot rag out of a pail of hot water and soak backs or necks if they were sore. "He'd soak cow's horns too and put two or three of them on the back of the neck or around the back. When he put a horn on the hot skin that had been soaking, the horn would draw up and raise the skin.

"Then he'd take a straightedge and make little holes in your skin, and put the horns back on again. The horns would draw up your skin and fill up with blood. After a while, the horn would drop off or he'd take it off [he knew when it was ready] and throw it into the water pail. Cupping took an hour or so; the horns worked really fast. He put Fels Naphtha soap on top of the cut and nobody ever had any infection. For three or four hours of massaging, he would charge fifty cents or a dollar. Later, maybe two dollars.

"Sick people would have to come in cars, but after the treatment they were well enough to walk home a quarter or a mile. They'd laugh and have a heck of a good time. It really was a miracle thing."

Though Jennie Laine of Brimson, Minnesota, had never been cupped herself, her father had needed a treatment as a young married man. "He said he started aching so, he ached from his head to his foot. It was just like a nerve ache or a toothache, all over his whole body. Whether it was a type of rheumatism or whatever, he said he even considered suicide because it hurt him so much," Laine recalls.

"Someone told him of an elderly woman . . . a *kuppari* from Finland. Dad went, and she did this cupping on him and drew out that blood, and he said from then to his old age he never had any rheumatism or aching."

Laine remembered a *kuppari* song her mother sang:

> *Jos mina taturi olisin*
> *Kupparin mina naisin*
> *Sattuis kuppari kuoalemaaen*
> *Sarvipuisin saisin . . .*

which she translated as: "If I was a *tarturi*, I would marry a *kuppari*. And if the *kuppari* would happen to die, I would inherit that *sarvi kosida*, that bagful of horns." Unfortunately, Laine couldn't recall what "*tarturi*" meant and had never asked her mother. (Mauri Haikola

Cowhorn used for cupping. This horn, belonging to Julie Pirnat, shows a deep groove in the small end for attaching the pig bladder. The size is in comparison to a quarter.

of Oulu, Finland, offered two suggestions: *parturi* is a barber, while *taituri* is a skilled person or magician.)

Miracles Lite

Finnish American settlers used the handy sauna for minor medical ailments as well. Salo recalled that "during the summer when the mosquitoes were bad, the sauna cured itchy mosquito and woodtick bites."

Esther Babiracki of Minneapolis, Minnesota, said that, when she was a child, her teacher sent a note home with her, saying she had head lice. "So mother took me into the sauna, and poured kerosene over my head. The smell was terrible." But she got rid of the head lice.

This bather discovered that her sunburn didn't hurt after a session in the sauna.

Sylvia Grampl from Graz, Austria, sunburned herself on a summer vacation to northern Minnesota. Though she'd been to sauna in her home country, "I did not endure the Austrian sauna very well," due to circulatory problems. Then she discovered that American saunas were more to her taste—shorter and not so hot. "I enjoyed it very much and felt very healthy during the time. This feeling became stronger with every visit in the sauna." So she wasn't going to give up a chance to sauna for a little sunburn. To her surprise, the next day her sunburn didn't hurt.

Not the Hair of the Dog!

Hangovers are occasionally treated with extreme remedies—like taking a hot sauna. Very few swear it works. Most prefer a milder cure, and wisely so. Some people still think the sauna cures hangovers. In "The Sauna and Alcohol" in *Annals of Clinical Research*, authors R. Ylikahri, E. Heikkonen, and A. Suoka, believe that a sauna while intoxicated creates a serious health risk. "During the hangover phase, the body is exposed to a heavy stress reaction. This is shown by the vigorously increased heart rate and cardiac pump performance, in addition with several hormonal and metabolic changes. Further, during hangover, sauna bathing and accompanying heat-induced stress reaction may further potentiate changes caused by alcohol and thus retard the hormonal recovery."

In other words, adding a hot sauna to a foggy hangover slows, not speeds, recuperation. Thus the sauna is the "place for whisks, not whiskey," Hillila says.

113

Hide Those Animals!

"They cured and waterproofed animal hides in the sauna," Salo says. "They put ashes in a tub, then the hides, and heated up the sauna until they could scrape the hair off. They made grease from pine tar, bees wax, and ear tallow. They heated the sauna and lubricated the hides with warm grease. You could walk through water in boots made that way."

The sauna helped pioneer families with other daily concerns. Edward Koski, of Brimson, Minnesota, says that "If you were in the woods and peeling, say balsam, and you got that pitch on, you had to take a sauna. That pitch was like glue that would stick to your clothes and everything. You couldn't get that stuff off unless you really rubbed it, or took a sauna."

The sauna wouldn't neutralize the skunk smell, however. Norman Rajala wrote in his journal of trapping a skunk and getting sprayed by it. "Mother made up a fire in the sauna, a hot one, too. She came in there herself to scrub me for sure with homemade lye soap, which also burned. No way could she get that smell out of my hair or that yellow [bleaching caused by the skunk spray] out of my skin and hair."

For Whiter Whites

The sauna was also used for doing laundry. Clara Carlson, of Brimson, Minnesota, remembers: "On Saturdays would be washday. We'd pump water from the well and haul it to the sauna (on a sled during the winter) and it would be heated there. That's where Grandma would wash clothes using soap rendered out of the fat from the pigs when they were butchered."

"We had a washing machine in the sauna porch," recalls Eino Kukko, of Brimson, Minnesota. "In the summertime, we always hung the wash outside because we always figured that the sun would bleach it and make it whiter. If it happened to rain, then we hung the wash in the sauna because we had a little heat remaining in there from the washing water."

Jennie Laine's mother kept the wringer and washtubs in the sauna, handy to the heated water. The sauna was also used by Laines as a summer kitchen. "Mother used the sauna porch for a summer kitchen when the days got real hot. Then she had a tiny little cook-stove in there, and she'd go and cook meals. That kept the house from heating up."

The old sauna had innumerable other uses: a place to wax skis, work leather, shape wood for furniture and implements, bend horse collars, sprout potatoes before plantings and for the hundred other daily household and farm chores.

No wonder Grandpa Ivar Rajala had tears in his eyes when he replaced the old *savusauna* with a new version with a chimney.

Chapter Twenty-Two

Savusauna Recipes
JUST A PINCH OF *LÖYLY*, STIR WELL

"Warm as a meat sauna." Finnish saying

Besides fulfilling dozens of household functions, families used their *savusauna* for cooking certain Finnish foods. Even without exact instructions, the adventurous can experiment. Others can just go hungry.

Talkkuna, a porridge-like food, was prepared from a mixture of rye, oats, barley, and peas boiled in a large cast-iron pot and dried on the sauna platform. This mixture was then ground and blended with clabbered milk. A *savusauna* (smoke sauna) imparted that special smoke flavor, Virtanan says.

What Kind of Pancakes?

Marvin Salo of New York Mills, Minnesota, grew up eating blood pancakes. After winter butchering, the blood from the animals was allowed to freeze. The sauna would be heated, the frozen blood would dry out, and when all the liquid was gone, the remaining blood would be saved, kept until the family needed protein. Water and rye flour would be mixed with the dried blood to make the pancakes. "Good too," remembers Salo.

Kalja, a Finnish home-brewed beer required malt, which was made in the sauna. Making the malt so it sweetened properly in the sauna required abundant skill. First the barley was put into a burlap sack and soaked in water (a stream if available). After two days, the sack was taken to a slightly heated sauna and left there. When the barley had sprouted well, it was spread on the platform and the sauna brought to full heat. For the next two days and nights, while the sauna was kept hot, the barley was stirred well and occasionally moistened so that all of the grains sweetened evenly.

Once the grain was dried and conditioned, it was ground into flour, ready for beer making. Some well-to-do farmers built separate malt saunas so they did not need to interrupt their regular saunas while making malt.

Smokin'

The mild heat of the *savusauna* cured meats and sausage. In the Great Lakes area, meat from deer and moose was smoked, as well as fish, and hams. After heating the sauna with juniper and alder-wood, people would hang lightly salted meat from the ceiling and place a dish directly under each piece to catch the melted fat. When the sauna was hot, the meat cured slowly, with a protective layer of smoke-scented fat on the surface of each piece, according to Virtanen.

To make sausage, Salo says, "First grind it. Then sew bed sheets into long bags two or three inches in diameter. Stuff the bags and tie the ends. Then you throw the bags in the wash boiler. Heat the sauna, and put the wash boiler in it."

Salo recalled a neighbor who had trouble with his batch of sausage. "This guy had the sauna going and was going to smoke that meat. So he gets it hot, and hangs it up on the ceiling, where it gets the hottest."

The cloth was all black (indicating the smoking process). But those sausages kept getting shorter and shorter. He thought somebody might be eating them. "Why are they getting so doggone small?" he finally asked. The answer was simple: he had overcooked the sausages.

It's too bad that most of the *savusaunas* burned down. Imagine the taste treats that would be available today.

117

Chapter Twenty-Three

Sauna Changes
SMOKE GOT IN MY EYES

It's a madman that bathes until his skin is scorched.
Finnish saying.

Whenever one person has a good idea, another will improve on it. The first sauna, a crude covered earthen pit with hot rocks and fire near the door, filled up with smoke; it served its purpose, but it was bound to be enhanced with new ideas.

For hundreds of years the place for sweat baths remained the same. Whether in a pit or a rectangular log cabin, people in different nations enjoyed variants of the sauna. Ibrahim Ibn Jakub, a Jewish-Arabian doctor, described the building and the practice in the border regions in Mecklenburg and Bohemia in about the year 972 A.D.: "Baths the Slavs lack, but they build a room of wood, the chinks they block with . . . moss. . . . In a corner of this room they build a fireplace of stones above which they leave an opening in the ceiling for the smoke to escape. When this fireplace has been heated, they seal the opening and close the door and pour water on the glowing fireplace so that steam arises. Everybody holds a bundle of [twigs with] leaves in his hands with which he stirs the air. And then the pores open and that which is superfluous in the body emerges from them and flows down along them in streams, so that no sign of rash or boils remains to be seen on any of them. And they call the house *al-atba*."

Original saunas looked like this one in Michigan. When chimneys were added to stoves, the saunas began changing. (Courtesy of the photo collection of Eva Seger, DeBarry, Florida)

The *savusauna* building and the process remained the same throughout history, according to the Finnish Sauna Society, until the beginning of the twentieth century. "The sauna had a single room with a stove and benches. Water was used sparingly, and the body was cleaned through sweating and using the *vihta* or *vasta* [birch whisk]. Rinsing and cooling was done in a lake or river if one was nearby, by pouring water over the bucket or by rolling in the snow in the winter." Water could be heated by dropping hot stones in a wooden container.

Oh, Too Bad

But the *savusauna* had disadvantages. The Finnish Sauna Society identified several: First, the *savusauna* took up to five hours to heat, plus another hour or so for the fire die out, smoke to vent, and the sauna to "settle." In a *savusauna* (and the early chimney-type sauna) the heating flames go directly through the stones, so bathing could start only after the fire had died down. This process could not be shortened, so preparing for the sauna was then an all-day experience.

A second disadvantage of the *savusauna* was the soot, which drifted from the open fire onto all surfaces inside the sauna. Scrubbing the soot off the platforms before the bath was a hot and dirty, but mandatory, chore. Ben Rajala remembers, "The benches and walls were coal-black from hundreds of baths, but once the top layer of soot was wiped off, the blackness never stained our skin."

But the major disadvantage, says the Finnish Sauna Society, was that smoke saunas easily caught fire. In Finland as early as the seventeenth century, officials prohibited the building of a sauna near other buildings to diminish the fire danger due to the sauna fire.

Clara Carlson of Brimson, Minnesota, recalls one hot Saturday during haying season when her family's first log sauna burned to the ground. "Mom and I went into the woods with a gunny-sack and picked up old pine stumps and old pine knots. We carried them into the sauna and started the fire. Later, Grandpa looked out the window, and there was the sauna going up in smoke. The pine knots got too hot. So—no more pine knots in the sauna stove."

In the late ninteenth century, according to the Finnish Sauna Society, the stones were covered with a conical metal top connected to a chimney. The top part of this addition included a door that could be left open or closed to control the temperature. When open, bathers could throw water on the stones.

Fired, But No Fires

Then came steel sauna stoves. "The most popular stoves were enclosed barrel-like stoves, where there was a lid for *löyly*," says the Sauna Site. "The stove was heated before opening the lid to add steam."

These new stoves required only a couple of hours to heat and could be used almost immediately after the fire had died out. They were much easier to maintain, with no soot accumulation. But the greatest advantage was the reduced fire danger; thus sauna construction spread rapidly. According to the Finnish Sauna Society, "In the 1950s, about half of the saunas in Finland were of the new type," while the smoke sauna persisted in eastern and northern parts of the country. Often, the old smoke sauna was left to ruin and a new sauna with the chimney-type stove was built next to it.

"The changing needs of a new urban and industrialized population encouraged the new sauna stove design too," explains the

Finnish Sauna Society. "In the countryside every house could have a sauna, but in the city people had to use public saunas. Because urban sauna stoves had to have chimneys, people got used to this different kind of sauna."

Hmm, If a Guy Put the Fire over Here . . .

In the 1930s, another leap was made in sauna design. A tinkerer separated the fire from the stones and created a continuous burning sauna heater. Now the stones were held in a metal casing above the fire, with cast-iron elements to transfer heat from the fire to the stones. With this kind of heater, wood could burn during the sauna, and bathers could take a sauna with steam. The intensity of the fire regulated the temperature of the stones and of the entire room. Instead of the one to two hours required to fire up a barrel stove and get to sauna, it now took as little as twenty to forty minutes, so bathing could begin even more quickly. In addition, the new way was efficient in small saunas where barrel stoves were too big, took up much space, and heated more slowly.

The fire still had to be watched continuously. Because this effective new heater could easily heat the sauna very hot, some people missed the softer quality of the *löyly* of the older stoves. However, the practicality of this kind of stove has made it the most popular wood-heated stove in Finland, according to the Finnish Sauna Society.

Continuous-burning heaters took over after World War II. Mikkel Aaland, in *Sweat*, notes that "The disappearance of the *savusauna* encouraged the growth of Finland's sauna industry. Obviously, the *savusauna*, with its hundreds of kilos of rocks and logs, was not a marketable item. But the new, metal-cased stoves were."

Electric Saunas

Sauna technology adapted to the needs of urban populations with the invention of electric heaters, which took over in popularity in the 1970s and 1980s. Like continuous-heated wood-burning stoves, electrical resistors heat the stones instead of open fires. Because electric stoves are inexpensive and easy to use, a sauna can now be built almost anywhere. "Saunas had been relatively rare outside Finland until the 1970s," according to the Sauna Site, "but electricity made it possible to build saunas in the cities in places where the handling of open fire was strictly forbidden." Saunas could now be built in apartments, hotels, ships, anywhere.

However, the disadvantage was that early electric stoves often used too few stones. Because of the small amount of heat stored in the fewer stones, the sauna had to be heated quite hot, and thus *löyly* became drier and harsher. More stones require greater energy to heat them, but the stones give more pleasurable *löyly*, says the Finnish Sauna Society.

"In the best electrical stoves there are enough stones so that the water thrown does not make contact with the resistors, since that creates a bad aroma. Some stoves can even be used so that after the stones are hot, the electricity is turned off for the time of bathing."

Says the Finnish Sauna Society, "Generally, electrical stoves are not considered as 'good' as wood-burning ones. They definitely are farther apart from the original sauna, but it is also true that a good electrical stove is better than a poor wood-burning one."

Any source of energy can be used in a sauna—gas and oil included—but in Finland these are rare. Gas and especially oil may have the disadvantage of odor, which is strange to the sauna atmosphere.

Next!

Another attempt to improve electrical sauna stoves came with the introduction of a fan to circulate air inside the stove to prevent burning up heating elements, according to the Sauna Site.

Introduced in 1990, like a convection oven filled with stones, the circulating air spreads the heat from the heating elements to all the stones inside the stove. The fan warmed up the sauna quickly, in only thirty to ninety minutes depending on the capacity of the heating elements and the amount of stones.

Engineers and designers continue to work with manufacturers to improve sauna stoves, says Mark Raisanen of Saunatec, Inc., in Cokato, Minnesota. The heaters change to meet the need of a more demanding and sophisticated sauna-bathing public.

The Sauna Building

Old saunas consisted of a single room, which housed a stove and benches. Like the sauna stove, this building changed little for hundreds of years. Bathers cleansed themselves by sweating and using birch whisks within the room. They rinsed off in a lake or river, or poured warm water over themselves outside the room. (To heat water, bathers placed hot stones in a bucket of water.)

With the advent of higher hygiene standards, says the Finnish Sauna Society, "A container for hot water was added to the side of the stove or as a separately heated cauldron, and washing was done inside the sauna. In summer it did not matter, but in winter it was rather unthinkable to wash outside in the cold."

Two views of the Ray Laitinen sauna, unusual with two doors. The front door is seen at the left, and the other door at right. Built in 1910, this Finnish log sauna was donated to Ironworld by the Laitinen family, Iron, Minnesota, where it is being restored to its original appearance.

Before bathing, people hung their clothing on pegs outside the sauna, and sometimes returned from their bath with little or nothing on, so as to complete the cooling process, according to the Finnish Sauna Society. Now "hot rooms and washing rooms are separated, and with the chimney-type sauna, this style slowly spread into private saunas, too. After all, washing is more pleasant in a cooler room."

Thus began the separation of space, one place for dressing and another for the heating room. Later, a third space, a cooling porch was added, giving bathers a place to relax, enjoy scenery, conversation or one's own thoughts. "Starting in the 1920s many saunas had a porch and a separate dressing room. In summer cottage saunas, other rooms, such as a kitchen and a bedroom, were often added [to the sauna] if no other building was available for living."

Sauna floors changed too. While a *savusauna* floor was most likely plain, packed earth, covered with slats where bathers would step, the Finnish Sauna Society notes that, "The next phase was a floor built of boards, and ultimately floors are laid with tiles on concrete."

People nowadays might lament the passing of the *savusauna*. What they might forget is that their forefathers and foremothers were relieved with each new sauna improvement. They could enjoy their traditional bath that, in Malti Kaups' field notes reported in *Sauna Studies*, was cleaner, took less time and fuel to heat, looked better, didn't sting the eyes, and was better for the children.

Who could argue with that?

Part III
Tales Told from the Top Bench

Chapter Twenty-Four

Sauna in the U.S.
MAYFLOWER COMPACT—NOT A SMALL SAUNA

The "Saunaburger": The hamburger hot off the coals with "nothing on" but served with a "switch" of parsley and garnish in just the appropriate places. Salad comes with no fries.

Menu item at Beatrice Ojakangas' restaurant, "Somebody's House," Duluth, Minnesota, 1970s.

Napoleon's Josephine and the Spanish queen of Argon characterized Europe's abhorrence for the bath. Elizabethan lovers exchanged peeled apples they had worn under their armpits. Only a few nonconformists strayed, like the German eighteenth century poet Goethe, who had a passion for swimming. Goethe lost at least one friend who believed Goethe had misguided delusions about bathing and swimming. Sauna bathing was popular only in Finland, the northern reaches of Sweden, Russia, and pockets of Europe at the time when it reached America.

America, however, didn't follow Europe's lead. Colonists from Sweden and Finland arrived in North America only a few years after the *Mayflower*. The Swedish contingent, which settled in 1638 in the Delaware River Valley (now the Philadelphia Navy Yard), included Finns (who had to choose between life in the Finnish army or the new colony). According to Amandus Johnson, they built bathhouses;

an old inhabitant of Pennsylvania said, "in his youth [about 1665] almost every Swede had a bath house." These bath houses, built near a river, were like those in the mother country, primitive in structure, similar to the *pörte* or Finnish dwelling (also called *bastu* or *Finsk bastu*) described by Guiseppi Acerbi.

The Swedish and Finnish colonists cleaned and rejuvenated themselves with their sweat-bathing tradition—water poured over heated rocks to cause heavy perspiration, birch branches, a woman to assist in scrubbing, high platforms for bathers. Though the colony didn't endure, the first saunas left their mark in the United States. A core of the Swedish-Finnish settlement area remained there even after New Sweden incorporated into the nearby Dutch colony.

Until the 1860s, few Finns immigrated to the New World. But then, famines in Finland, fear of conscription into the Russian army, and Norwegian ore mine depletion caused as many as 400,000 new settlers to immigrate to North America between the 1850s and 1920s.

They found the Lake Superior area similar to the old country in appearance and climate. In their communities and farms in Michigan, Minnesota, Wisconsin, North and South Dakota, and Ontario, they continued their sauna-bathing tradition. Homesteaders built their own saunas, often the first structures to be built on the farms, and used them also as houses, living in them until cabins could be built.

Ma, Look-it There!

The first sauna constructed in Minnesota in 1868 caused a lawsuit, according to Florence Barberg Merrill, of Cokato, Minnesota, in her family history. Neighbors Barbo (later Barberg) and Selvala built a sauna

on the boundary line between their farmsteads, Merrill writes, "a log building ten by twelve feet and seven feet to the eaves. It had no

This, the oldest *savusauna* in Minnesota was moved to its present, Temperance Corner, location north of Cokato.

This sign commemorates the site of the first *savusauna* in Minnesota in 1868, located north of Cokato, Minnesota.

This is the door of the oldest *savusauna*. It had a variety of closures, which included a rope latch. The door, like the corners of the building, is interlocked and angled for strength and water drainage.

dressing room or windows but had two openings in the wall for smoke to escape. The elevated bench at the side wall was four feet from the floor with another bench along the side wall, with a stepladder, a chair and a wooden wash tub." These neighbors took turns heating the sauna every Saturday through the year, all the families bathing together as was the custom. The sauna served the families for over twenty years.

"In the late [eighteen] seventies, the line through the center of Section 18 became the public road. Our sauna was located right in the center of it. Seeing the naked bathers amused other nationalities passing the sauna.

"In the mid-eighties, the township road was laid there and the sauna was ordered to be moved. [By then] Selvala had acquired Barberg's share. The town board refused to allow any compensation for its removal and only three dollars for damage to the right of way. This was unsatisfactory to Selvala so he sued the township, won the case and was awarded thirty dollars for the damage and forty dollars for moving the sauna. However, the sauna got wrecked in the moving, so he built a new sauna on his farmstead."

The interior of the sauna at the Cokato museum, showing the long johns some bathers donned after their sauna. The *vihta* hangs from one wall, while a bucket, a dipper, and two varieties of homemade soap rest on the *laude* (bench). (Courtesy of the Cokato Historical Society Collection)

Settlers on the Great Plains found few trees on the prairie; innovative Finns built saunas from improvised materials. With no timber, Andrew Haarmala built a sod house from the thick prairie turf in Newell, South Dakota, writes Gene Tuura, of Edmonds, Washington. Over time, he acquired the critical items to make a sauna out of his soddy — a stovepipe, a window, and a couple of doors.

Suitable fuel was the next problem, and he solved it by using "Bucking Annie," similar to the buffalo chips. "With the cattle [*Haarmala*] had going in and out of the ranch," Tuura says, "he had a factory for fuel. After experimenting with this new-found fuel source, he determined that he could only use it from cattle that fed on range grass, since it burned clean like straw briquettes without an offensive odor." Haarmala then crafted a special wheelbarrow for his children to collect Bucking Annie over all his prairie pastures so the family could once again enjoy their saunas.

Several hundred Finns homesteaded on North Dakota farmlands and began communities like Rock Lake and Wing. Like other neighbors, Joseph Luukkonen, who arrived in 1902, promptly built the sauna, which cleaned and rejuvenated his family hundreds of times over the decades. Grandson Howard Carlson remembers the day when both he, a very young child, and his grandfather Luukkonen, then in his nineties, watched others build a new sauna with a chimney.

For Finns who lived in towns, public saunas sprang up to fill the need, according to Matti Kaups, of Duluth, Minnesota, in "From Savusaunas to Contemporary Saunas." In *Sauna Studies*, he describes Calumet, Michigan, newspaper ads promoting public saunas for Finns and non-Finns alike, the best of which in 1888 in boasted "separate sections — dressing, washing and sauna rooms — for men and women." Townspeople of all Finnish communities — the Lake Superior region, from New Jersey and Florida to Oregon and California — used the indispensable public sauna.

Even so, most Americans knew little of the sauna unless they lived in a community with Finns.

The Winner Is . . . The Sauna!

In the late 1920s when Finnish athletes began competing worldwide and winning, Americans sat up and took notice. Paavo Nurmi, the "Flying Finn," won nine gold medals in three Olympic competitions, setting track and field world records. Because of his exploits, Americans read of the saunas that Finnish athletes advocated as part of their training.

More Americans caught on when Finnish athletes competed in 1936 Berlin Olympic Games. In "The Sauna as a National Symbol," Pekka Laaksonen writes that Finnish athletes brought a sauna with them. Using a specially designed stove and logs from an old drying barn, athletes reconstructed the sauna on site. They also brought sauna whisks, believing that "German bathing whisks could not be counted on." While many curious spectators and athletes observed, the Finnish athletes went on to win. The success of the Finnish runners was ultimately attributed to the sauna.

When the Winter Olympic Games were held in Squaw Valley, California, in 1960, Americans took another look at saunas. The sauna concept started making sense to the uninitiated.

In 1961 a visit from Finnish President Urho Kekkonen converted President John F. Kennedy. When President Kekkonen yearned for a sauna, according to H.J. Viherjuuri, "Cecil Ellis drove his 'saunamobile' demonstration unit to the residence of the Finnish Consul General in Pelham, New York to be placed at the service of the distinguished guest." President Kekkonen enjoyed it and explained the intricacies to President Kennedy, who found some relief for his back pain. Says Mikkel Aaland, "Later, President Kennedy and his family enjoyed a sauna in the White House." The following year Vice President Lyndon Johnson journeyed to Finland and was introduced to the sauna. The sauna boomed in America.

The prototype Finlandia Sauna, built by carpenter Harold Dorr for Ben Rajala, Finlandia Sauna president in the 1960s. His daughter Kitty Rajala demonstrates to a prospective (but fully dressed) customer how water and the *vihta* might be used.

Kind of Like a Sauna . . .

Though Americans with Finnish ancestry understood sweat bathing, the complex traditions of the sauna were not immediately grasped by other Americans. Advertisers linked products like facial steamers or weight-reducing pants that used heat or steam to the healthful sauna. Sometimes the process wasn't understood by the Americans who installed saunas in their homes. Karen Rajala, of Cohasset, Minnesota, enjoyed a sauna in her Chicago home during that time. But not knowing how to actually take a sauna, she used it only to warm up her children after swimming.

Other times, the building itself was poorly constructed. Though it looked pretty, one home sauna had "orange crate benches and seeping pine walls."

Eager to take advantage of the new trend, American hotels and gyms installed saunas. They misunderstood the need for super-hot stove with rocks, so they didn't have rocks, concerned for the safety of their inexperienced-in-the-sauna guests. Sometimes the stove was heated with few rocks. Some stoves weren't hot enough. At some saunas, putting water on the rocks was prohibited. Cleaning people didn't know how to properly maintain these saunas.

The sauna, a "new" status symbol, had its ups and downs in those years. Montgomery Wards and J. C. Penney sold saunas through their catalogs in the 1960s. According to Matti Kaups in *Sauna Studies*, "only 14.5 percent of the 1,061 motels, hotels, and resorts in the states of Minnesota, Michigan, and Wisconsin listed in the tour books of the American Automobile Association have saunas" in 1974 and 1975. Sauna hit a downcurve when used as a front for prostitution businesses.

But eventually the reputation of the Finnish sauna was secure. Now, in America, one can find saunas at sports establishments, summer and winter camps for kids and adults, at health clubs and gyms, upscale hotels, day spas, and rehab clinics. Saunas, both old authentic versions and new adapted ones, are introduced to thousands of Americans each year. Once people discover the joys of sauna, they keep on taking them.

Dear Mom, Camp Is Great. I Took a Sauna!

Howard Carlson of Rock Lake, North Dakota, says, "A sauna is a wonderful thing because it extends the lake season. When the weather is cool, if you get cold when you're swimming, you can come in the sauna and warm up. Once you get good and hot in the sauna, you feel like jumping in the lake again. Once the neighbor kids try it, they want to build one of their own."

Concordia College of Moorhead, Minnesota, sponsors language camps for young people, including a Finnish one. At Salolampi, the Finnish Language camp, students learn sauna etiquette, and are "required" to take one sauna during their two-week session, "just to get the experience," according to camper Maia Bentz, age eleven, of St. Cloud, Minnesota. "We could also do it during free time when we go swimming. Since it was right by the lake, whoever went into the lake went in the sauna before and after. I [took a sauna] three or four times when I went swimming. It was a nice way to warm up before going in the lake and get all dried off after."

These children (left) can use the sauna to warm up after swimming in the lake at Salolampi, Concordia's Finnish Language Village. Language campers learn sauna etiquette and customs during their stay. Most continue to enjoy saunas after their one required session (right). (Courtesy the Concordia Language Villages)

When a porcupine found their sauna to his liking as well and chewed some of the steps and benches, the Salolampi counselors promptly made up a Finnish "porcupine song" to teach their campers.

Like many homesteads, Salolampi's sauna was the first building erected at the camp. It stood idle until volunteers remodeled it and added a Finnish stove and benches; it has been used as well during other language camp sessions for Swedish and Russian camps.

YWCA Camp DuNord on Burntside Lake, near Ely Minnesota, has a large log sauna. Since it was built before there were roads in the area, the logs were floated down river to the camp site before construction began. Wally Nippolt of St. Paul, Minnesota, and a Camp DuNord camper for thirty-seven years, estimates that 3,000 to 4,000 new families were introduced to authentic saunas over the years. His most memorable sauna was a winter sauna "when the wind chill was ninety degrees F. below zero. We steamed up in the sauna [close to 200 degrees F.] and jumped in the lake. We had earlier cut a hole in the ice and put a two by four across it, so that when you jumped in, you'd have something to pull yourself out with. You went in with stockings because if you did not, it would take the flesh right off the feet." Mostly Nippolt prefers more moderate saunas, "where you can sit on a bench outside after the sauna very comfortably for five or ten minutes in the spring or fall and enjoy the crisp air and the stars."

Bible camps introduce saunas to their campers too. In North Dakota, Bruce Carlson of Velva says that a camp his church sponsors, Metigoshe Bible Camp, "wants us [two or three Lutheran churches] to build another sauna, a bigger one, next summer. We've put three or four there so far, some by the water. But so many kids use the saunas that they wear them out."

Camp Hiawatha, a Bible camp near Deer River, Minnesota, recently built a sauna near the lake with wide cooling decks in front. An outer deck, with lawn chairs, allows campers and counselors a great view of the lake with or without taking a sauna. Inside is a screened and roofed area, equally pleasant for sitting or storing wood.

Masterpiece

The Scandinavian Heritage Park in Minot, North Dakota, displays a sauna as both an authentic work of art and a working sauna. Bill Koski from Phelps, Wisconsin, hand-hewed the logs with his son-in-law and intricately joined the corners. Koski and his son-in-law demonstrated these skills and explained sauna heritage to festival visitors at FinnFest 1997.

Alfred Juntinen (left) of Rolla, North Dakota, and Howard Carlson (right) of Rock Lake, North Dakota, cool off outside the specially-commissioned sauna in the Scandinavian Heritage Park in Minot, North Dakota. The stained-glass window behind them (not visible) is a replica of the Finnish flag. (Photo courtesy of Bruce Carlson of Velva, North Dakota)

"The sauna was hot every day during FinnFest 1997, so visitors could feel the heat and smell the pine," says Bruce Carlson. "The people who enjoyed it most were the folks from Finland, specifically the Finn entertainers who took saunas the traditional way while visitors stuck their heads in out of curiosity."

While the physical work was done by Phelps and his son-in-law, people all over North Dakota with Finnish ancestry contributed building pioneer memorials to fund the building. And it's still a working sauna. "We heat that sauna whenever we have Finnish activities, like the planning meeting for Host Fest, notes Carlson. "We had a picnic a month ago, and the sauna was hot."

Suit or No Suit?

Maplelag, a cross-country ski resort in Callaway, Minnesota, has several saunas, some of them in old log buildings that owners Jim and Mary Richards have relocated to their resort. Maplelag boasts a "suit sauna" and a "no-suit sauna." John Hooper of rural St. Joseph, Minnesota, preferred the "no-suit" sauna when he and his family spent a weekend skiing a few years ago. Hooper remembers, "My youngest son, Dylan, and I would go into the sauna after we'd had a hard ski workout. Sometimes, there were three or four others, sometimes just my son and I. We'd get it very hot and go roll in the snow once or twice. Then [we'd] go back in the sauna until we couldn't stand it anymore, and then come back out.

"I heard that the owner would cut a hole in the ice, but nobody had done that while I was there. I definitely would have jumped into a hole in the ice."

In Grand Marais, Minnesota, a sauna is part of the community public pool and recreation area. It is big enough for twelve to fifteen people to sauna, and since it is mixed, males and females together, swimwear is worn. Instead of throwing water on the rocks, bathers pull a string to dispense the water. To cool off, people can sit outside or take a shower. A few might even jump in the pool.

The monks of St. John's Abbey at Collegeville, Minnesota, own property near Bemidji, Minnesota, with a sauna. The buildings didn't include a sauna when it was donated to the monastery in the

Smoke indicates that this winter sauna will soon be in use (right). This sauna (at right and above) is located on St. John's Monastery property northwest of Cass Lake, Minnesota. It was probably once a stable. Father Richard Eckroth converted it into a sauna. (Courtesy of Charles and Evelyn Eckroth of St. Joseph, Minnesota)

137

1920s. One decaying log cabin, possible a stable, was patched up by Father Richard Eckroth and transformed into a sauna. After the stove and rocks, says sister-in-law Evelyn Eckroth of St. Joseph, Minnesota, he fixed up the porch, and an outhouse. "We'd come here [in the 1970s] and share the place with mosquitoes, mice, and squirrels. Our kids loved it. It was primitive and not much used."

Since then the monks have renovated the property, and added electricity, new cabinets, and a giant sauna. Though it's used often now, Father Eckroth looks forward to an occasional retreat there and to taking a sauna.

A Barrel of Fun

A far cry from either old log buildings or the early prefabs are the barrel-shaped saunas built by Jack Rozycki of Rice, Minnesota, which add a unique dimension to American saunas. "For the last twelve years, we've built saunas with the traditional methods of a cooper—no nails and no glue," says Rozycki. "Each white cedar stave is cut individually with an arc and a bevel. We steam-bend all the staves and bring them together with hoops. Then we pound the hoops until it's a barrel and as tight as a drum. Once it's aged, it's water tight, and cracks won't form. It doesn't need any other roof.

Cooper and carpenter Jack Rozycki of Rice, Minnesota, gets ready for a winter sauna in his backyard. Each stave of his white cedar barrel sauna is individually cut with an arc and bevel. (Courtesy of Jack Rozycki)

Another Rozycki barrel sauna (top). Note the cooling porch and plunge tank. Interior (bottom) of Rozycki Cooperage and Manufacturing in Rice, Minnesota, where barrel saunas are built. The unique shape is produced by banding, pounding and steam bending each stave. (Courtesy of Jack Rozycki)

"We use an elliptical shape on our barrels because it's a nicer, more useful space. The height and width are better proportioned when it's elliptical. Inside, all curved lines lead to the floor drain, the bunghole. There aren't any flat spots to collect moisture or mildew."

His Rice, Minnesota, cooperage gets requests for his elliptical barrel-saunas from Minnesota and Wisconsin and as far west as Colorado and Washington.

Most of his saunas use Finnish-built Polar electric stoves, because they're easy, fast, clean, efficient and inexpensive. Buyers could opt for a custom-built, wood-fired Four Dog stove, which feeds from the outside to keep the smoke, ash, and litter away from the interior, says Rozycki.

The World's Only Sauna Reggae Band

Sauna provided the inspiration for another unique project. Les Ross, of Negaunee, Michigan, founded the Finnish reggae band, Conga Se Menne. He says, "It gets so cold in this part of the world where we live that you have to do something to warm up. You can only take so many saunas to do that," says Ross. "You need sauna music to take you away from the cold. We've found that hot sauna and warm Caribbean sounds provide enough spirit and sun without our having to fly to St. somewhere."

So the group wrote lively songs with an island beat that feature the sauna and life in Michigan's UP (Upper Peninsula).

With these and other Finnish reggae music, the group Conga Se Menne serenaded those entering the World's Largest Sauna at Finn Fest '96 in Marquette, Michigan. In an attempt to set a world record, organizers had erected a huge tent, bleachers, and jet butane heaters (and arranged for sweltering weather). While the event didn't quite achieve the record, the sauna participants did "the wave" and enjoyed an otherwise fine sauna with live music.

It is a measure of how far the sauna has come in America, that it can be so cleverly mentioned in a menu, as Beatrice Ojakangas did, assured that everyone will recognize what a sauna is.

Chapter Twenty-Five

When We Were Children

I DIDN'T DO IT!

"A lot of the kids don't take time to build a sweat lodge. They just go downtown and pay a couple of bucks to take a sauna."
George Watchetaker, Cheyenne

The sauna means different things to children than it does to adults. Children struggle to understand the meanings their parents sometimes place on it. For example, the rocks look like any old rocks. Right?

Janet Rajala Nelson of Minneapolis, Minnesota, recalls a summer day playing at her Grandpa Ivar's house, waiting for her father and uncles to stop talking. When she and her cousins had run out of other amusements, they began playing in a new play house—the sauna. "After a while we wanted to build things. Since we had no materials, the sauna rocks became our blocks. We moved those rocks all over the place, in and out of the sauna."

That was the day Janet discovered that sauna rocks were special, not toys, and definitely not to be moved. After all, the rocks had come "from Finland." Though she can't recall the exact punishment, she and her cousins were severely reprimanded.

141

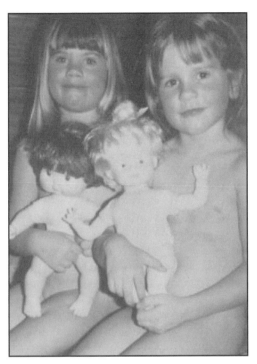

Emily Rollie (left) and Saara Jalonen aren't too young to enjoy a sauna. (Photo courtesy of Jude and Bob Jalonen)

A barrel-shaped sauna is appealing to this young boy.

A Guy Thing

After splashing water on the rocks, perhaps splashing something else comes to mind. Janet's brother Tom Rajala of Cohasset, Minnesota, remembers that as a kid, he and his cousin Brian sprinkled the rocks with a different fluid, urine, just before they left the sauna. "The adults seemed to know what the smell was. They came after us quick." Tom notes blank spots in his memory when asked about the reaction of the adults when he and his cousin were caught.

Richard Asiala, from Traverse City, Michigan, tells of his children's same urgent need but a different solution to the problem. "On a winter afternoon, my brother, his daughter, my two boys (all five or six years old) and I marched through eighteen inches of snow out to the sauna. We undressed and went into the *pessä*. Sauna was hot. Brother and I were ready. Almost at once, one of my sons said, "Dad, I have to go [pee]." Annoyed, I said, "Go in the drain." My other son followed with, "Dad, I have to go." I repeated, "Go in the drain." Brother's daughter said, "Dad, I have to go." He said, "Wrap a towel around you and go in the house." Out the door she streaked to the house—with the towel wrapped around her head.

Dear Lord, Please . . .

Mary Wade, of Kenosha, Wisconsin, found her first sauna experience at age ten somewhat bizarre, but it wasn't the sauna itself that so amazed her. "Being the modest person I am, I put my bathing suit on, and I went in there with my grandma and my little sister. My grandma took it naked," she recalls. "What I remember most is this is the first time I ever saw my grandmother with no clothes on. She was very well endowed, and pretty old, at the time. She had these humongous breasts that hung down to her waist. I thought, "'Dear Lord, don't let mine look like that when I get that old.'"

Parents found special ways to bring their small children to the sauna during the winter. Ruth Norha Anttiila of Virginia, Minnesota, remembers that all of the kids and her mother took their saunas at the same time. One by one, her mom carried the children back to the home in a blanket. On cold winter days, she remembers their hair would freeze before they got back inside.

That first sauna as a child can indeed be an indelible experience.

Chapter Twenty-Six

Sauna Hospitality
SHAKING HANDS WHILE NAKED

"Two places are holy – church and sauna." Finnish proverb.

After Americans took note of the amazing Finnish athletes in the 1920s and 1930s and their "secret weapon," the sauna, an editor of a large city newspaper tried one himself. In an editorial, he described his experiences, "The Finnish sauna is not a solo performance in washing up—it's like a meeting. It reminds one of campfire gatherings in the olden days."

Handcrafted decoration identifying and welcoming bathers into the sauna is a common form of sauna artwork.

Saturday night in the sauna was not just the time for cleansing the body. It was a traditional get-together for neighbors and relatives, and the social event of the week. Some families were renowned for their warm welcome. Bernice Carlson of Rock Lake, North Dakota, remembers the times with relish. "The wonderful thing in the Finn culture is the hospitality. Around this area, you'd just go and visit and have a sauna. Then we would have head cheese and homemade bread and homemade million-dollar pickles. My husband Howard's cousin was so hospitable that everyone wanted to go there for sauna. His wife always made this homemade head cheese, on homemade bread. It makes my mouth water right now."

Please Pass that Wonderful (Head Cheese, Cake, Bread)

Sauna company was part of the usual routine on Saturday evenings on the Karjala farm west of Menahga, Minnesota. Now from Winona, Minnesota, Jeanette Karjala recalls, "Guests would begin arriving about 7 o'clock. We [the children] had to be in and out of the sauna well before that. After the sauna we looked forward to treats— orange juice and biscuits. And then it was bedtime by 7:30 in the evening! Upstairs in our bedrooms, we could hear the indistinct adult chatter and laughter as the adults awaited their turns.

"My younger sister Lorraine and I were assigned the task of mixing and baking three cakes each Saturday—one yellow, one white, and one chocolate, based on memorized recipes. For some reason, we prepared white frosting for the chocolate cake, chocolate frosting for the yellow cake, and butter frosting for the white cake. The cakes must have been tasty, since the sauna guests kept repeating the ritual for years."

If the food was special, the sauna company made the occasion even more so. Lillian Barberg, of Cokato, Minnesota, writes in her family history, "Usually a dozen or more large, flat loaves of bread were baked and sometimes a batch of coffee biscuits, doughnuts, or big fat sugar cookies made from sour cream for sauna company. Sauna company was always served coffee, too; otherwise the 'cooling off' would not be complete.

"During this cooling off period and coffee-drinking time, stories were told. While the women were in the sauna, the men sat around smoking, drinking coffee and spinning yarns. The ghost stories were the favorite ones. Because of them, the children hardly dared to make their trip out of the sauna into the dark on their way to bed."

Eva Seger of DeBary, Florida agrees. "To be invited for a sauna bath of a Saturday night was almost a social affair. My folks knew many of the farmers, so we were frequently invited for sauna. After everyone had his turn in the bathhouse, the lady of the house served hot coffee and Finnish coffee breads. I think what I enjoyed most was the lively conversation that followed. Their stories were so exciting, I didn't want to go home."

Come On In!

Bathhouse night was busy for the families who hosted them. "Our sauna was heated every Wednesday and Saturday, the most popular day being Saturday," remembers Effie DeKeyser of Gladstone, Michigan. "We [as kids] had to gather cedar each Saturday in our area to make the *vihtas*. Most of the older guests said it was necessary for a good sauna."

"Many friends came carrying their towels to our house to enjoy the steambath. We provided the soap, plus after the sauna, my mom served coffee and food in our home. Most of the guests gave my mom money, usually a dime per person. No price was ever mentioned or asked for, but that amount was customary. Our sauna was in use for seven to ten hours each Saturday. It was a definite social activity.

"As my three sisters, two brothers, and I grew older, we didn't want to 'get in line' to get into the sauna. We'd appeal to our mom to stall a guest so we could take a quick bath. [My sisters and I] discussed many things in the sauna—boyfriends, school, lessons, Luther League projects, you name it! The sauna is where a girlfriend explained the facts of life to me, when I was at the ripe old age of fifteen or sixteen.

"Some sauna-goers were in and out in a half hour while others enjoyed a leisurely hour. One favorite guest was Reverend Heimonen. Even in his old age he would stay in the sauna for hours.

In fact my mom would become worried and send my dad into the sauna to check on him. He was always rosy and smiling after all the *löyly* he'd enjoyed. He probably planned many a sermon there."

Big sauna gatherings on Saturday nights are rare these days. Still, here and there the tradition continues. "We used to go over to this one family's sauna every second or third Saturday night," says John Hooper of Cold Spring, Minnesota. "Sometimes it would be just two families or a potluck, where the kids would play and we'd sit in the living room or kitchen and talk. Sometimes there'd be larger parties, with a sauna."

Those good times with friends in the sauna are what Conga Se Menne, the Finnish reggae band from Negaunee, Michigan, sings about. "Sauna Song" tells of a guy who's worked hard all day and is ready to relax—in the sauna: "We rink a beer or mebbe two. . . . We get the steam go, yump in the snow. It would be much neater if I beat you with the cedar bough, it makes the blood flow." In "*Soumalainene Boika* Blues," a lonely fellow misses the social aspects when he takes his sauna alone and wishes to find a young damsel to share his sauna. Two songs, "Guess Who's Coming to Sauna" and "Look Who's Sitting in the Sauna" tell of the legendary snow deity, Heikki Lunta, a special guest.

The sauna is the place to relax and enjoy companionship with friends or a quiet moment alone. (Photo courtesy of Saunatec, Inc.)

These are songs the Conga Se Menne band still sings to its audiences in northern Minnesota, northern Wisconsin, and much of Michigan, today, Les Ross says, reminding people of sauna days past, and suggesting even better sauna days yet to come.

Chapter Twenty-Seven

The Public Sauna

SEATING ARRANGEMENTS

Finnish Bath House
on Monroe Street
John Kantoniemi, Prop.
Steam Baths on Saturdays
from 1:30 to 11:30 P.M.
20 cents
including towel
Everything Clean.
                    Eveleth Mining News, 1904

Public sauna was a common fixture in the urban areas of Finland. When immigrants arrived in the United States, the idea of the public sauna immigrated with them.

The first public sauna in America opened in Calumet, Michigan, in the 1870s, according to Matti Kaups in *Sauna Studies*, and served Finns in copper mining areas. By 1879, a newspaper reported ten "nice genuine" public saunas in Calumet for the 754 Finnish-born residents of the township and neighboring counties. Bernhard Hillila wryly wonders if Finns who applied for work in what was known to be a "sweatshop" might have thought it was a public sauna.

The concept of the public sauna quickly spread after its first United States introduction. By 1895, according to Kaups, when Finns arrived to work in iron ore mines, public saunas began to operate in the Iron Range communities of Minnesota. Thunder Bay, Ontario, Canada, boasted five public saunas. Finns across northern Minnesota went to "bath house" in Duluth, Hibbing, Grand Rapids, Coleraine, International Falls, Eveleth, and Ely. Public saunas were used from Lake Worth, Florida, to San Francisco, California. They spread from the Finns to other groups as well.

"My husband, Wayne Koski, and I used to go to the Virginia Public Sauna on Friday nights before we bought it," recalls Harriet Koski Erickson of Mountain Iron, Minnesota. "Mainly families with children came, and couples. But there were groups, too. By the time we took the business over, every nationality was coming, predominantly Finnish, but also Italian, Irish, Jewish. For at least ten years, on Friday afternoons, a group of lawyers came. Some were Finn but most were not. Later in the evening, the college kids used to come in. They all liked having a sauna.

"We had chairs in the lobby for people waiting for a sauna. Sometimes it was so busy in the summer that they'd wait on the steps outside in order to get a chair inside to wait. We were open Tuesday, Friday, and Saturday. In the winter, some people came every time we were open. At first, a sauna in the public room cost fifty cents, and maybe a dollar when we quit [twenty-two years later]."

Erickson fondly recalls those days, "It was lots of work, and we used to get tired, but we really enjoyed it. We got to know so many nice people."

Built as a public sauna in 1911, the Virginia Public Sauna operated for seventy-five years before closing in 1986. The last owners faced restrictions, liabilities, and increasing costs of power.

Public Sauna Hijinks

Ben Rajala, from Grand Rapids, Minnesota, visited Tervo's Sauna in Grand Rapids, which was a big, clean place. Because the benches were made of cement, they were often slippery. And sometimes he ended up with a skimpy towel. He remembered owner John

Tervo as a person who liked to play tricks. "He'd go in with you and get it real hot. It would get so hot I had to lay down to find cooler air. One time Tervo left suddenly. I was laying there relaxed. Then, the door flew open, and Tervo sloshed us down with a bucket of water with snow in it! I screamed to high heaven."

Art Hongo charged twenty-five cents at the public sauna he owned in Calumet, Minnesota. His rule, no beer, was subverted by a group of high-school friends who hid their six-packs of beer in the snow outside, and took turns bringing in beers. During the sauna conversations, one young man confessed to having a crush on a local beauty named Loretta. He could not see well without his glasses, and when it came his turn to go out and get more beer buried in the snow, he started outside wearing neither towel nor his glasses. Just as he fumbled his way outside in the altogether, his buddy sitting on the bench inside shouted, "Hey, isn't that Loretta? Hi, Loretta!" Mortified, he whipped around and stubbed his toe so hard he broke it. And come to find out, it wasn't Loretta after all, or even a woman, just his trick-playing buddy.

It Keeps On Going, and Going . . .

The Ely Steam Bath in Ely, Minnesota, is one of the few public saunas that has remained opened when those across northern Minnesota have closed. Now owned by Richard "Slim" Ahola, the business has been in the Ahola family since it opened, "My grandfather built the place in 1914, and I started working here in third grade. I sat behind the till and gave out towels. The Ely Steam Bath is the oldest family-run business in Ely."

"We're open three days: on Wednesday and Friday, we open at 3:30. The sign says 4:00, but you've always got to open early for the early birds. On Saturday, it's 1:30 (though the sign says 2:00). That way they feel like they're special. We let them in until 8:30, but then they have to get out by 9:30. Restaurants close at 10:00. I've been here since opening, so I have to get something to eat."

There's both a men's side and a women's side, and two private rooms besides. "New people are always coming. On Wednesday, it was two couples, one from St. Paul who'd read about the Ely Steam Bath in a book."

Ely resident, Bob Jalonen, visited Ahola's sauna every Wednesday and Saturday. "Slim Ahola always made the visit special as he got to know you. He would learn what kind of topics and anecdotes you enjoyed and would share one or two on the way in or out. He is what makes going to the Ely Steam Bath so special."

"Going there routinely got you settled in to paying attention to where you sat in the public men's room (I assume there was a "seating chart" on the women's side also). It was considered prudent and customary to attend at the same time so you could be assured of being with the same fellows and keeping up with the on-going stories.

This Space Reserved

"The men's dressing room had benches around the perimeters, with a set of benches running down the middle of the room. There were pegs every foot or so along the wall and between the two sets of benches in the middle of the room. Many pegs had "reserved" designations on them. Pity the poor man who hung his clothes on a designated peg. A cold shoulder, at best.

"After leaving the dressing room, you entered the shower room, which consisted of about ten or twelve shower heads. Each shower head had its own personality. Veterans know which ones to [use] because of the volume and intensity of the spray. Neophytes ended up with the "dripper" type.

"Heat (in the steam room) is applied by pulling a rope which permits water to fall onto the radiators. No greenhorn, tourist, or young person was permitted this honor. You had to earn the right to do so, and only did it when given permission by the most senior group. The old timers would enjoy turning up the heat by having the rope pulled and watch the neophytes slowly cook. It seemed like the new guys would always head for the top shelf to prove their manliness, and it was great fun to watch them slowly slink down to the lowest bench, the bottom-most of three tiers.

"There was a faucet with hot and cold running water in the hot room and the shower room. Many of the guys would take one of the black, rubber pails and fill them up with water to splash themselves with and/or to soak their feet in. It was considered customary

151

and mannerly to wash off the bench where you sat with this water so that the following occupier of that particular place wouldn't be seated at the same spot your bare butt just occupied.

"The stories that would ebb and flow from the old timers were always a delight to me being interested in the history of the area. After spending fifteen to thirty minutes in the hot room (until one felt like a limp washcloth), you stepped back into the shower room and washed up with soap. Your pores had been opened by the heat and the dirt and grit were sweated out, and now it was time to really clean those pores out. This was followed by a cold, cold shower to close the pores and rejuvenate one's body by lowering the body temperature from a 100-degree-plus back to 98.6, or cooler. Then into the dressing room for a cold one, or two. It was here that most of the gossip, lies, and truths were told.

"Most would go back for a 'second shot' in the hot room, followed by the cold shower. After that, one cooled down some more, gossiped some more, toweled down, dressed and headed home after bidding 'adieu' to your partners and designating if you would *not* be present the next designated sauna day. If you did not designate that you would be absent, it was assumed you would be there."

Learning the Ropes

Tom Schwichtenberg discovered Ahola's on his third day of studies at Vermilion Community College in Ely. Schwichtenberg thought he was going to a "saw-na" similar to motels he'd stayed at. Instead he found the rich social tradition and great camaraderie in talking to another generation. "They kind of liked seeing me, a youngster in my twenties. They thought it was nice to see the youngsters enjoying the tradition. Finns, Scandinavians, and Yugoslavians, they'd sing a couple of traditional songs in another language."

One day Schwichtenberg sat with a logger and learned about *vihta*, the pliable leafy twigs used to increase circulation. "The logger told me that he had once used alder leaves, but was too old to collect them outdoors. Besides, he said the branches would only last a month or two. He'd upgraded, to these plastic pompom things on a stick, which had lasted up to five years. He told me how to make the real ones with alder branches. This guy was the only one who still did that. The others [said they] did when they were younger but not anymore."

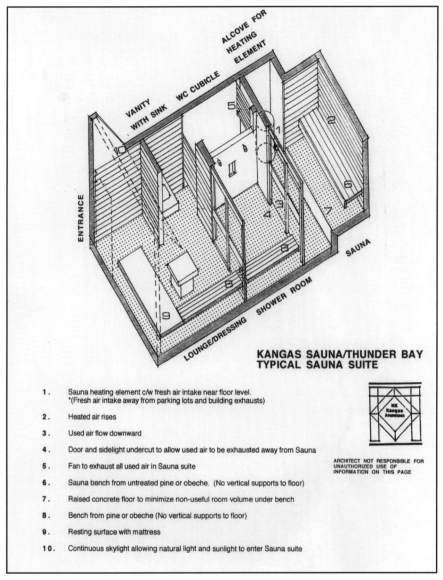

**KANGAS SAUNA/THUNDER BAY
TYPICAL SAUNA SUITE**

1. Sauna heating element c/w fresh air intake near floor level.
   *(Fresh air intake away from parking lots and building exhausts)

2. Heated air rises

3. Used air flow downward

4. Door and sidelight undercut to allow used air to be exhausted away from Sauna

5. Fan to exhaust all used air in Sauna suite

6. Sauna bench from untreated pine or obeche. (No vertical supports to floor)

7. Raised concrete floor to minimize non-useful room volume under bench

8. Bench from pine or obeche (No vertical supports to floor)

9. Resting surface with mattress

10. Continuous skylight allowing natural light and sunlight to enter Sauna suite

KK
Kangas
Architects

ARCHITECT NOT RESPONSIBLE FOR
UNAUTHORIZED USE OF
INFORMATION ON THIS PAGE

An architectural drawing of a typical sauna suite at the Kangas Sauna in Thunder Bay, Ontario, Canada. Kalevi Kangas, the architect, designed the benches to have no vertical supports to the floor. A skylight allows natural light to enter the sauna suite. Air flow for heating and ventilation was carefully included in the plan.

State of the Art

In contrast to the long-time public saunas is a relative new-comer, the Kangas Sauna in Thunder Bay, Ontario, Canada, a unique and beautiful public sauna, full of daylight, glass and natural wood. Kathy Kangas manages the Kangas Sauna, started by her mother Lyyli in 1967. Kathy says, "There were five public saunas in Thunder Bay when we first opened up, but they weren't very attractive. They were a service for the Finn community. Ours is the only one left. I'm not sure it will last, but it's been open now for thirty-three years,"

Designed by her brother Kal Kangas, an architect, the Kangas Sauna is a family project. It began with eight private sauna complexes, each one with a dressing room, shower, and sauna room. "We got a lot of publicity both for the food and for the saunas," remembers Kathy Kangas. "We had a lobby and a ten-stool coffee bar, which served hamburgers and strawberry shortcake to those who were waiting. The wait for saunas were up to two hours at the beginning."

Since then, Kangas recalls, they've expanded four more times and now offer seventeen private suites. In each addition, the sauna rooms have gotten larger. Now they include five medium sauna suites and four large sauna suites, each with a private bathroom, double shower and skylights. Medium saunas hold up to eight people, but they're not restricted only to larger groups. "Sometimes a person or couple takes a medium just for the luxury of a private bathroom and only a few extra dollars," Kathy says.

You Are Invited . . .

Two of sauna suites have conference rooms. Kal Kangas says "They're very popular for someone getting married. On a Saturday, the groom and his friends come and get ready for the wedding. Suites are rented for birthday parties and the Superbowl so patrons can watch the game."

Kangas Saunas added a hot tub in a tropical setting with a skylight above. And the adjoining restaurant now has fifty seats. "We serve an awful lot of Finnish pancakes with strawberries and whipped cream. On weekends, the restaurant is full. Lots of people go sauna first, then they have the meal," says Kathy Kangas.

Who visits the Kangas Sauna? Since the Finnish people often have saunas in their homes, says Kangas, "Tourists come, and native Indians, families, couples, people on shift work, people who may not have great facilities to bathe in at home or where they're renting. Eighty or 100 a day came on very busy days."

Kangas Sauna never advertises, partly because of the struggle against the negative image some saunas obtained in larger cities. "We try to keep a clean and respectable image. We've had to fight to do that. Our reputation could be destroyed if we were usurped by the wrong crowd. Suddenly the families wouldn't come, and our business would be ruined.

"We're busiest in the winter and on weekends. It's very reasonable to take a sauna. For one person, the regular size sauna is nine dollars; for two, $13.00, for an hour and a half. We are open seven days a week, all year round, except for two weeks and statutory holidays."

Though many sauna-lovers have their own saunas in their homes, public saunas serve the need of friendship and camaraderie with people outside the home.

Chapter Twenty-Eight

One-of-a-Kind Saunas
ALL SAUNAS ARE NOT CREATED
EQUALLY

"After the war with the Soviet Union from 1939 to 1944, the peace agreement dictated that Finland had to pay a large amount of compensation. Much of it was paid in the form of ships (which helped the Finnish shipbuilding industry and the economy of the whole country.) Some of the ships were warships, and according to some stories, the Russian generals and colonels wouldn't accept wood as bench material for shipboard saunas. It was not durable enough. So, the Finns did exactly as they were told, and built metal benches for the Russian shipboard saunas."

Legend recounted by Mauri Haikola

Necessity, being the mother of invention, has spawned an immense variety of extraordinary saunas. People need to put a sauna in a complicated location, like the Arctic Circle or up a steep hill or on an island. Or maybe someone wants to relocate one for a short time, for hunting or fishing perhaps. Maybe people just want to keep their saunas when they move. Those saunas won't look much like typical saunas. They'll be unique. The materials will be unique — like a car or ice blocks. Every now and then, someone conjures up a truly beautiful sauna. The creators of the saunas in this chapter showed great imagination and fun!

A group of young Finnish men created a sauna in an unused car to prevent it from being sold or hauled away. The heater is in the trunk, and the passenger seats were taken out and replaced with benches. Extra insulation was added to prevent heat loss from the interior. The record number of bathers who steamed up at the same time in this car sauna is twelve.

The Mobile Sauna

In the summer of 1993 in Heinola (which means arrogant town), Finland, a group of young men faced the unpleasant prospect of dealing with a car standing idle in the backyard. They could comply with either of two authorities. The owner of the backyard (and mother of the car owner) where the car had been standing said, "Scrap it." The City Council Facades Committee said, "Move it."

The young men chose neither. Instead they decided to make the car useful again by building a sauna into the vehicle. To do so, they installed a stove in the trunk of the car, removed the wall between the trunk and interior and replaced the usual passenger seats with benches. To increase their bathing pleasure, they added a radio cassette player and a cell phone.

After several nights of construction, the young men enjoyed their first steam in their "mobile sauna" in June 1993. Due to humidity, however, the cassette player shorted out and no longer works, but the car still runs, according to website <www.eskimo.com/~juha/mobile.html> and <www.students.tut.fi/~w119586>. "In midsummer 1997, we broke the packing record: twelve people bathing at the same time in the sauna-Renault. The atmosphere was tight, as I recall." (Perhaps both literal and slang definitions of "tight.")

It's Not a Boundary Waters Trip without a Sauna

John Holm, of Tower, Minnesota, used a similar creative approach to materials and location when he and his friends constructed a portable sauna for Memorial Day weekends. Using the truck portage from one lake to another enabled them to tote increasingly heavy gear. When faced with difficulties, they modified and upgraded. Holm's story is a case study in creative problem solving.

"In May of 1978, I started going on an annual Trout Lake fishing trip ("fishing trip" is sort of an exaggeration.) The truck portage was still open, so we didn't pack light: cooking gear, cots, large tents, and kegs of beer.

"In 1978, we had a particularly wet weekend. What we did all weekend was sit around the campfire and drink beer. It was a miserable trip, but it didn't dampen our spirits.

"Before the trip in 1979, I got some seven-mil plastic from work and my partner (Gene Heikkinen) and I made a large tarp. To do this we put newspapers on a picnic table, overlapped the pieces of plastic, and, topped with a grocery bag, ironed the seams together.

"The tarp was to sit under in case of rain, but, lo and behold, we had beautiful weather. Although the weather was warm, the water was cold, so swimming was out of the question and washing up was a cold and miserable experience.

"Then Gene had a brainstorm: why not make a sauna?

"We decided to tie rope around three trees that formed a triangle and drape the tarp over it. Then we dug a pit in one corner. Since we didn't have a stove, we piled large rocks on the fire grate

158

and heated them up for several hours. When they were hot, we used a washpan to transfer them to the sauna.

"Then ten of us stripped down and crowded into our makeshift sauna with a bucket of water. There was a lot of steam and the plastic did a good job of keeping the heat in. When the rocks started to cool, we all soaped up and dove in the lake. While this served the purpose, it also got us thinking on how to improve it.

"In 1980, we used the same tarp and constructed a crude framework out of aspen poles. We also brought an old wood stove someone found laying around. The stove was rather heavy so we hid it in the woods to use again the next year.

"In 1981, we made a framework out of ¾-inch PVC pipe and form-fitted the plastic over the five-foot-high, five-foot-deep, five-foot-long frame. When we got to Trout Lake that year, much to our dismay, we found that the Federal Forest Service had discovered our stove and removed it. That year, without a stove, we had to improvise and boil water on a Coleman stove for steam. It served the purpose. The five-foot-by-five-foot sauna was roomy enough to put four lawn chairs in. For a doorway, we cut a slit in the plastic, and draped another piece over it. When wet, the draped-over piece would seal both sides of the slit.

"In 1982, we used the same basic setup, but changed the framework to conduit, with four-by-four-inch blocks with holes drilled into them for corners. We also bought a small fishhouse stove and converted it to hold rocks on the top. This served us well until the truck portage was closed and we could no longer carry all our gear."

The Post-Sauna Leap

Neil Gardiner, who lives on Beatrice Lake, in northern Minnesota, used the same brand of imagination when he built a sauna on a hill thirty-five feet up from water, and a long wooden slide to get there. Bathers at his sauna, when ready to jump in the lake, could grab one of the plastic sleds stacked near the door, hop on, and slide right down into the water. As Greg Breining says in an article for *Sports Illustrated*, "The particular strength of that technique was that there could be no changing of the mind once the body was set in motion."

A barrel is a unique but comfortable shape for a sauna. All water easily drains to the bottom.

Unfortunately, Gardiner no longer has that sauna. Built with a boathouse permit, it didn't meet the required distance from the lakeshore. He removed it due to zoning regulations but plans another one inside the basement of his new log cabin.

No Corn Allowed

Neil Gardiner's neighbor, Harold Rudstrom, on Big Sturgeon Lake, Minnesota, built a sauna thirty to thirty-five years ago out of half a wooden silo. "My friend only wanted half of the silo, so I took the other half and made a sauna. It was a lot of work but I've enjoyed it more than anything I have out here," Rudstrom remembers.

"This silo was clear two-by-six fir, tongue and groove on the inside and wrapped with tar paper on the outside. It had three and one-half inches of redwood siding on the outside, which is spiraled on the sauna," Rudstrom recalls. "It's not straight across and I never realized it until I was cutting it in half. When I got to the other side of the silo I found I was one board off."

After cutting, Rudstrom had to move the silo-sauna to his cabin on Big Sturgeon Lake. "I almost lost the whole thing. The rope broke when we were trying to lower it to the ground and the silo fell. When it falls, a round wooden thing like it looks just like a rubber band laying on the ground.

"I tried to haul it over to the island, roll it over after using chains, hoists, or cables inside to solidify it and make it round and try to roll it over. That was too much work. I ended up rolling it up on what was going to be a pontoon boat and put about a half dozen empty propane tanks under it. Then I brought it up the shore. I'd cut long tamarack poles and put them down by the dock and pontoon

160

Harold Rudstrom built his sauna from half a silo. It's visible here from the top of his woodpile. (Courtesy of Harold Rudstrom)

boat and winched the silo up. When it was in position, I cut the tamarack poles away and dropped it down on my joists.

"I built a changing room on the side. If I had known my friend was going to tear his half apart just for the lumber, I would have got his half to make my changing room. My barrel stove feeds from the outside so I don't get birch bark, sawdust or wood chips inside the sauna.

"I was going to make the benches completely round so it would be impossible to corner a woman, but I gave up on that idea. One nice thing about this sauna is that you have enough floor space to get down and wash. It's too big (at thirteen feet in diameter) to heat up for myself but I do anyway.

Says Rudstrom, "I've had as many as eighteen people in there, but they were all nude. If they had swimming suits on you could never get eighteen people in there."

The Miners' Delight Arctic Sauna

A sauna for a 1981 gold excavation project in Eagle, Alaska, (seventy-five miles south of the Arctic Circle) was just as arduously planned and moved. "The sauna was the best thing that ever happened. You could have hot water and get clean," Tom Rajala, of Cohasset, Minnesota, remembers. "Even though a creek was nearby, nobody would go in it. The temperature couldn't have been more than thirty-four degrees F. It started flowing in June, and froze in August. Karyn, my wife, tried it one time but never again."

Sam Rajala, Bud Siegel, and Tom Rajala of Cohasset, Minnesota, included a sauna among the buildings in their gold camp. They asked Ben Rajala, of Grand Rapids, Minnesota, to design seven or eight buildings, places to sleep, eat, cook and store food and machinery, each about eight feet by twelve feet.

"I started planning on Wednesday night, and loaded the materials, all cut and bundled, on the following Saturday morning," recalls Ben. "The materials were trucked 5,000 miles to Eagle, Alaska, plus seventy-five miles upriver from Eagle, and then pulled in a dray behind a Cat train over roadless terrain. This had to be done in late February when the ice was thickest on the river."

As best they could, workers at the camp then assembled the buildings, which had to be put on skids to keep them off the ground. Most buildings functioned well enough, but the sauna had a few problems. Concerned about overheating the wood floor, workers first laid rock on the ground, and then put the fireplace on top of that. It

The portable sauna designed by Norman Rajala and enjoyed by grandson Russ and his family. (Courtesy of Jim Rajala of Grand Rapids, Minnesota)

worked but still wasn't quite right.

In early August, Norman Rajala, of Coleraine, Minnesota, arrived at the Gold Camp. Norman's visit in Alaska was his first, and though he might have chosen to photograph the incredible sights or explore on his own, his first activity was to improve the sauna. After he heated it up for laundry and saunas, he discovered imperfections. "It needs lots of changes as they put it together way wrong," wrote Norman in his journal. Over the next few days he lowered the sauna benches, and made a door between the dressing room and sauna. Then he added two shelves and a "Finlander latch" on the outside door to keep it shut. Finally, it was just right.

A Little More to the Right

Norman Rajala, an inventor in his own right, had decided he needed his own sauna years before, in 1966. It had to be portable, so that he could move it around the country. He passed it on to son Jim Rajala in 1974, who used it for years and in 1997 passed it on to his

Many people need to move their saunas. Richard Luoma moves the mobile sauna belonging to him and his brother Jim Juoma onto county-leased land for hunting season every year. Because of strict regulations, this sauna had to meet requirements such as size, siding, and color. (Courtesy of Elvie Luoma, Makinen, Minnesota)

son Russ and his wife, Kathryn, of Cohasset. Now Norman's two great grandchildren enjoy saunas two or three times a week. It's still in wonderful condition. And every time they heat it up, Grandpa Norman smiles at them, says Jim.

A Tiki Sauna

Most saunas look like saunas, but the world's only tiki sauna belonging to Les Ross, leader of Conga Se Menne, the Finnish reggae band, does not. Though the inside parts are conventional, on the outside it looks like a tropical island cabana, with corrugated tin and thatched roof. "It looks like a hut you'd see on a deserted island," says Ross. "Plus it serves a dual purpose. The changing room, for example, has chairs inside and out, and also a large window. If you open the window, it becomes a tiki bar, with bar stools. You can sit in its shade or out of the rain. Or you can take a sauna." Ross's tiki sauna is still under construction.

Igloo Sauna

Connecting the opposite extremes of temperature, two young men created an ice sauna. Jukka Lappalainen and Seppo Toivanen of Rautavaara, Finland, assembled four walls with a couple hundred ice blocks and roofed it with snow. For benches, they set three rough planks on ice blocks stair-stepping up one side. Insert stove and bathers, and *löyly*, and steam. Literally. A substantial cloud of steam is rising from their ice sauna. To check it out, visit the following website: <wysiwyg://8/http://www.geocities.com/Athens/Acropolis/1895/jaas2000.htmp>.

Though others solve knotty logistical or engineering problems, or use distinctive materials, very few actually garner prizes. The sauna owned by Peter Kerze of Eveleth, Minnesota, won a prestigious architectural award after he hired architect David Salmela of Duluth, Minnesota. The architect built a double-duty bench inside, enlarged the windows, spiffed up the siding, and added a board walk to the lake. Voila! Usually fancy public buildings win, or extravagant homes. But this time, the winner was . . . a sauna. The list of original saunas grows daily. Some are beautiful, some are crazy, but each one is unique, which makes them all the more fun.

Chapter Twenty-Nine

Sauna in Finland Today

MEANWHILE BACK IN THE MOTHERLAND

News Flash! This just in.
The first annual "Sauna Bathing World Championships" were
held this weekend. Here now from Heinola (in southern Finland
to our world-wide audience, and incidentally the same town

One young Finnish man douses his head to cool off after heating up in a "mobile sauna" built into a Renault. The car is still driveable.

1666

where the car sauna was described in Chapter 28: One-of-a-Kind Saunas).

Sixty competitors, fifty-seven Finns. The men's division boasted fifty-two contestants, while the women's division had only eight. The championship winners had to stay in the sauna as long as possible. (By the way, this event was neither sponsored nor condoned by the Finnish Sauna Society.) Just a group of hearty, fun-loving, very competitive Finns.

The rules: to remain sitting, conscious and able to walk out of the sauna when they'd had enough. Contestants who lowered their heads to their knees were immediately disqualified.

The organizers kept the sauna temperature steady at 100 degrees Centigrade, and dispensed a half liter of water every thirty seconds. The competitors didn't throw any water on the rocks (or anywhere else) themselves, so rivals couldn't personalize this contest.

The women's winner survived in the sauna for about thirteen minutes. The man stayed nine minutes longer, an incredible twenty-two minutes. Two new World Records. You read it here first, folks, the first-ever World Sauna Championships from Finland.

True Love

This true story illustrates how the Finns love their saunas, in nearly infinite varieties and locations. Sauna is not just a tradition, but a way of life in the small Nordic country, and its popularity continues to increase. The Finnish Sauna Society estimates there are 1.6 million saunas in Finland today, triple the number from 1938. One sauna for every three Finns. In fact, Tim Bird writes in *Blue Wings*, that Finland is the only country in the world with more saunas than cars.

Mauri Haikola of Oulu, Finland, says, "Practically all houses in Finland have a sauna these days. In urban areas, you can usually find a sauna in each building, but even in a relatively small apartment, a sauna is not a rare luxury. Modern saunas have room for three to six people at a time, plus the usual shower and dressing rooms. Electrically heated saunas are common due to their safe, easy and clean use. Traditional ones near a lake or sea do not require anything but a stove, fueled by wood, and a bench to sit down on—you do your cleaning in the lake."

Saunas are everywhere in Finland. At hospitals, on passenger and cargo ships and car ferries, in hotels and motels. The possibility of a train sauna is being investigated. Nearly every apartment building has its own "house sauna." Saunas are found at swimming pools, gyms, sports centers, holiday centers, and camping sites. Factories and businesses maintain them so that their employees can enjoy monthly sauna nights with their coworkers.

Sauna Politics

Government included. Even the Parliament building in Helsinki has a sauna, used regularly by the members of Parliament and their guests. The late President Urho Kekkonen often negotiated in the sauna and perfected his renowned diplomacy there. He hosted important Soviet politicians and other guests of state in his sauna. His home, Tamminiemi, now a museum, had a sauna which must have contained a *laude*, or bench, of power.

In 1958, the Finnish Cabinet began "night school," the group sauna that completed their weekly cabinet meetings. That was possible when every cabinet member was a man. The tradition changed recently when women were elected to the cabinet.

Hot Tips During Steamy Shows

Since government leaders used saunas in real life, TV and radio picked up the idea and developed separate programs for their audiences. One of the most popular television shows in Finland used a sauna as their set. Among the show's guests have been a dozen cabinet ministers and nearly a hundred members of Parliament—usually towel-clad, of course.

Haikola describes the series: "Called '*Hyvät Herrat*' (Gentlemen), the show was a humorous and ironic look at the Finnish political life. The main characters were Mr. Paukku, a rich, fat, arrogant (but still, oh so lov-

167

Top: from the Finnish television series *Herrat Nauraa*, "Mr. Paukku" (right) expounds on his theory to world famous conductor, Mr. Okko Kamu (middle). "Minister Kolkivuo" (left) looks on dubiously. (Photo courtesy VIP Enterprises, Finland)

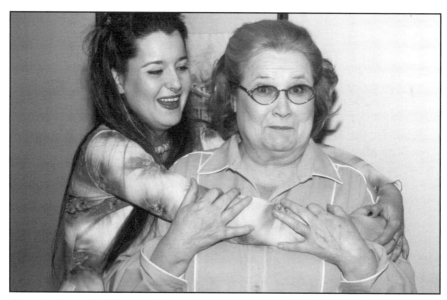

"Rosa the Waitress" (left), from *Herrat Nauraa,* who is the "Minister's" secret illegitimate child hugs "Washing Lady Tyyne Hurskainen" (right), who looks surprised at what she's just heard from Rosa. (Photo courtesy VIP Enterprises, Finland)

able) businessman who had somewhat questionable standards, like brib-
ing politicians when it suited him. He had a habit of bathing in a hotel
sauna every week with his son-in-law, Mr. Koskivuo, a member of
Parliament (who later in the show became a cabinet minister).

"In every show, there were one or two guest stars who were
prominent MPs or other politicians, sports people, or any kind of real-
life celebrities, playing themselves. They too went into the sauna with
Paukku and Koskivuo, and I guess that is what made the show so
popular.

"Most of the show's dialogue centered on Finnish day-to-day
politics. An elderly washing lady in the hotel sauna pampered the
guests and always had some clever insight into the current politics as
well as the history behind it. You had to watch this show if you wanted to keep in touch with the latest rumors and behind-the-scenes
political talk (in the real Finnish government), like before elections.
The show's writers were quite experienced political journalists."

The series aired more than 100 programs, the last of which
were named "*Herrat Nauraa*" (Gentlemen Laugh).

Not Just Hot Air

A Helsinki radio station opened up its sauna to people with
opposing views about current events. As debaters aired their opinions, the station recorded it, right in the sauna. The show was called
"*Lauantaisauna*." Saturday Sauna became very popular. Why did it
work? According to L.M. Edelsward in *Sauna As Symbol*, "Because
Finns are more open when they are naked."

Since a session in the sauna dissipates anger, it allows people
to reach agreements through compromise. Government and media
know this. So too do Finnish businessmen who use sauna bathing for
their commercial negotiations. Many international business guests
discover the custom when finalizing a deal in the company sauna.

However well it works, Finnish business women may feel dis-
advantaged when they are excluded from sex-segregated business
saunas. Says one woman quoted by Edelsward, "Those stupid business saunas, they normally make women's progress and presence in
a welcoming work community more difficult."

The Consummate Sauna

The Finnish Sauna Society maintains an excellent sauna establishment near downtown Helsinki but in a natural setting. They heat four genuine wood-fired saunas—two *savusaunas* and two saunas with chimneys. In addition, their facilities include an outside porch, the opportunity to swim in the sea (regardless of season), the services of a washing lady, a masseur, or a hair dresser for women, a cafeteria and lounge, a sauna library, office, and conference rooms. In the Finnish tradition of having different sauna hours for men and women, they reserve Thursdays and Mondays for women, and other days (with some exceptions) for men. This time allocation is based on the relative number of each gender in the membership.

Meanwhile, Out in the Country . . .

Saunas proliferate in the Finnish countryside. Most every lake or river or seashore is dotted with hundreds of thousands of summer cottages, each with its own sauna. One is unlikely to find a lakeside without a sauna.

Finns are so hooked on saunas that when they leave town as immigrants, sportsmen, or exporters, they bring them along. Olympic athletes lug a portable sauna from site to site, while Finnish soldiers build a sauna at each new base. More impressive than merely having a sauna, Finns actually use them. On average, more than once a week.

While on vacation at the summer cottage, many vacationers heat the sauna every day. Finns bathe in midweek, if they've had an extra-difficult day, when they're about to start a trip or when they return from one. Finns relax in their saunas at the end of a work week so religiously that the electricity grid suffers from distinct peaks every Friday and Saturday evening, when hundreds of thousands of saunas are heated, Mihael Cankar says.

Auld Lang Public Sauna

Saunas in Finland have definitely changed. Some sauna connoisseurs still enjoy the "real" smoke sauna, with soot-black benches and smoky atmosphere, and consider the *savusauna* superior in enjoyment and aroma, well worth the extra time and trouble it takes to heat them. While Finns might prefer steam from a wood-fired stove (the heat from an electric stove being dry and characterless), nevertheless electric and chimney-equipped stoves have almost completely taken over.

The need for public saunas declines as personal saunas increase in homes and apartments, and as businesses and sports centers have their own saunas. Though more numerous, saunas are becoming smaller, says Edelsward. "The standard is fast becoming the apartment sauna, or "mini-sauna," also sometimes called a "bathroom sauna" or, by the less enthusiastic, a "sweat closet."

Smaller dwellings with private saunas in each apartment become the norm. Mini-saunas rarely seat more than two or three persons comfortably, which means even families cannot all go to the sauna together. The days of large family saunas or large communal public saunas have past. Changes in size, therefore, affect the social uses and functions.

Finns love their saunas. The Finnish Sauna Society established a semi-official celebration "Sauna Day" on the second Saturday in June. The Finnish postal service issued a postage stamp to commemorate the chimneyless log sauna in 1977. Finnish authors since the *Kalevala* was written describe sauna in their books; sauna appears as a motif in paintings, and Finnish composers create songs about sauna. Saunas are set in Finnish films.

Sauna even plays its part at Christmas, when the Christmas sauna remains a major sauna tradition. "In my family," recalls Mauri Haikola, "We mostly go to sauna the day before Christmas Eve. Other people choose different times for their saunas—the morning of Christmas Eve, Christmas Day—depending on their family traditions.

Perhaps Finnish sauna traditions have loosened and are no longer greatly revered, but perhaps it doesn't matter, because in the end it's clear saunas are widely accepted, widely-used, and widely-loved in Finland.

171

Chapter Thirty

Sauna in War, Peace, and Diplomacy

During the Winter War, 1939 to 1940, Finnish troops near the front lines in Eastern Karelia believed Russian troops were reasonably distant, so a group of soldiers took their turn in a field sauna. While these men were relaxing and steaming up, Russian troops overran Finnish positions, and the front line of battle changed. Though the soldiers in the sauna didn't realize it, the rest of the Finnish troops had wisely and hastily retreated.

The first inkling they had of anything wrong was when they came outside to cool off. They discovered they had been left behind, without weapons, equipment, and worst of all, clothes. They were completely naked, as their clothing had disappeared. The dugout in which they left their equipment had been destroyed.

Then, in the distance they recognized the unmistakeable sounds of — Soviet tanks! Suddenly they realized, naked or not, they were actually behind the Soviet front.

However, they were not as distressed as one might think they would be in this untenable situation. There was still the sauna, so they ran back into the sauna for a round of löyly and some creative problem-solving. Later that night, they sneaked out of the sauna in small groups — and fled into the forest.

For two days they struggled through peat bogs and thickets, naked and becoming very scratched, until they found Finnish

lines, and then their unit. Their commanding officer promptly ordered a reward for the exhausted soldiers — off to the sauna!
Adapted from Businessman's Guide to the Finnish Sauna

Not only has the sauna been used for cleansing, rejuvenation, birthing, and cooking for the family, but the military used saunas in the tenth century, according to Johnson and Miller in *The Sauna Book*, where they report a tale from *Nestor's Chronicle*: a community is besieged by its enemies. Finally, in near surrender, they offer the dreaded enemies a sauna. While the enemies are inside, enjoying the heat and relaxation, a woman named Olga torches the sauna, and rids her community of their threat.

Experience, the Best Teacher

Long before the Winter War of 1939 to 1940, when temperatures dropped to bitter lows, the Finnish Army used saunas to warm their frozen soldiers. Finnish Field Marshall Carl Mannerheim ordered saunas built everywhere soldiers were quartered — in bunkers, dugouts, deserted buildings, and even in tents. John Virtanen says in *The Finnish Sauna*, "Mannerheim realized the Finnish soldiers were fighting on two fronts — one was a battle against the overwhelming power of the numerically-superior Russian soldiers with their armored vehicles, and the other was against the ever-present cold." The sauna alleviated the second of those enemies.

"Service regulations prescribed sauna once a week and in wartime soldiers often went to great lengths to arrange for their baths," notes H. J. Viherjuuri, in *Sauna: The Finnish Bath*. "Soldiers passing a sauna would light the stove so that those following behind could use it."

You Louse!

During wars, body lice become a major problem, and the sauna provided a solution for that as well. The Finnish army developed a portable sauna housed in a tent to double as a de-lousing station. While a soldier bathed, his clothes were placed in this special cabinet, which was heated to 180 degrees. By the time the soldier was finished with his bath, his clothes were effectively rid of vermin. This improved upon the old practice of hanging clothes over a beam near the roof of a *savusauna* to make use of the disinfecting powers of the smoky bathhouses.

The wartime sauna had to be built quickly, so it may have looked crude, Virtanen says. "Architectural beauty was secondary. Aerial camouflage was primary. Troops on the move had to be satisfied with tent saunas." Other units rebuilt abandoned saunas when they found them. Underground saunas were built whenever possible.

As might be expected, Finnish soldiers relaxed often in the sauna during the static phases of war. But they also enjoyed sauna even when they were in forward battle positions, like the men who escaped from behind Soviet lines. Virtanen says "With the whistling sounds of shot, shell, and shrapnel passing close overhead, the soldiers frequently prostrated themselves for protection, but never left for safety, as they thawed their frozen bodies in the 200-degree heat of the sauna."

This mobile sauna was used by Finnish Peacekeeping forces in Bosnia in May 1997. (Courtesy Secretary-General Urpo Rannansuu, Finnish Ministry of Defence, Information Section)

Note the cooling benches outside this UN sauna built on a truck and used by Finnish Peacekeeping troops in Bosnia since 1996. (Courtesy Secretary General Urpo Rannansuu, Finnish Ministry of Defence, Information Section)

Peace from Finland: Saunas for the U.N.

The sauna proved to be of such value among the troops that it continues today to strengthen esprit de corps and create unity. Finns serving as United Nations peacekeeping troops build a sauna at every base they occupy. "Since 1956 [in the Sinai and Suez] the Finnish peace-keepers have always built saunas in their camps. In Lebanon since 1982, over 500 peace-keepers have served," says Secretary General Urpo Rannansuu of the Ministry of Defence, Information Section. "In Lebanon there are over twenty saunas: several in the Headquarters area and every observation post its own sauna. In Bosnia, 500 peace-keeping Finnish soldiers have been stationed since 1996. In Bosnia the troops have quartering in the Camp Jussi so that twelve saunas are enough. In Kosovo, the 800 Finnish peace-keepers went late August 1999 and founded the Camp Ville. The first saunas were 'hot' within two weeks."

This "sauna oven," is used at Camp Jussi in Bosnia, where 500 Finnish Peacekeeping troops are quartered. (Courtesy Secretary General Urpo Rannansuu, Finnish Ministry of Defence, Information Section)

One of the twelve saunas used at Camp Jussi. (Courtesy Secretary General Urpo Rannansuu, Finnish Ministry of Defence, Information Section)

"The building of saunas varies with circumstances and surroundings," explains General Rannansuu. "Of course they use available local buildings and materials, if they are suitable. However, usually peace-keepers take saunas with them when they leave Finland.

The sauna and cooling porch of the battalion commander at Camp Jussi in Bosnia enclosed by a traditional fence. (Courtesy Secretary General Urpo Rannansuu, Finnish Ministry of Defence, Information Section)

Lebanon. A beautiful sauna built for the battalion commander. (Courtesy Secretary General Urpo Tannansuu, Finnish Ministry of Defence, Information Section)

177

There are two main types of saunas: dismountable timber-sauna and so-called "Rapid House" sauna, which is made of wooden prefabricated units. A specialty is the mobile-sauna, which is built on a truck. Sauna ovens are warmed up with wood, electricity, or heating oil. Close by the sauna is a water tank (used for fires), which at the same time is used as a swimming pool.

"In principle the sauna today is the same as years ago, and it is still very important to soldiers. The importance of the sauna described maybe best [in] that the sauna will be built immediately after quartering is done."

What is the sauna mainly used for? Says General Rannansuu, "It depends on situations and what soldiers need. Cleanliness is obvious. Then maybe relaxation and social intercourse are important in those circumstances. Finally, it's to feel good: You have a good hot sauna. After the sauna, you sit outside on a mild evening. You are clean and relaxed. You have a couple of beers. You talk with your buddies—it is joy and pleasure."

"It's certain that they will build saunas in the future, wherever they serve. The sauna abroad is a piece of Finland."

These saunas brought a bit of home to soldiers in a far-off country. Could the sauna also be the tool for softening two opposing sides in a war? Perhaps, according to Mikkel Aaland, who describes saunas he took with Finnish forces in Cyprus. Though the summer days rose to forty-three degrees C (about 110 F), the sauna was amazingly refreshing, due to the drop in temperature from the superheated sauna to the outdoor air. One sauna sported machine gun bullet holes, which actually improved the ventilation, according to the company commander. In fact, he reported that the "Finn's ambition was to build a single . . . sauna for the both the Turks and Greeks and be free to go home."

In a sauna, soldiers recover from rigors of battle, are cleansed, strengthened, rejuvenated, banish loneliness (or boredom during slack times), get rid of vermin infestations, and maybe even promote peace.

The Sauna as a Secret Weapon

The benefits of the sauna—relaxation and clear-headedness—aided peace negotiators as well. Bernhard Hillila quotes a Finnish couplet: "Anger cools in the sauna, Resentment fades away." Thus, sharing a bench with others makes a person feel less like arguing and more like agreeing. Moral obligations of honesty and good faith weigh more heavily on the participants than during formal negotiations.

Carlton Hollander, in *How to Build a Sauna* writes, "The Finns respect the sauna to such a degree that their ministers of government often conduct business in and around the sauna. The Finns believe that a man, upon leaving a fulfilling sauna, will be clear of mind and untroubled. They feel that by conducting business with people who have achieved this state, they will be able to deal sensibly and rationally with the matters at hand."

The Economist defined the sauna as "the secret weapon of Finn diplomacy and business life" in a January 9, 1988, article announcing the end of the long-standing group sauna following the Finnish government's weekly cabinet meeting once women were elected to the cabinet. (Men and women sauna separately unless they are family members.)

Prominent leaders both of Finland and other nations enjoyed *löyly* in the sauna of longtime President Urho Kekkonen. As President of a country tugged between America and Union of Soviet Socialist Republics during the Cold War, Kekkonen's visitors included both Vice President Lyndon Johnson and Soviet leaders. When he greeted the VI International Sauna Congress in 1974, Kekkonen shared his philosophy of sauna: "It is the great leveler. There are no ministers, VIPS, laborers, or lumberjacks on the sauna platform, only sauna mates. For me, as for most other Finns—the sauna is a way of life. In the heat, I forget the workaday stress and can meet my friends and acquaintances."

During recent decades, sauna bathing has assisted business and commercial negotiations in the same way. In the less-formal atmosphere, a freer exchange of viewpoints brings about mutual understanding. Sauna makes it easy for people to come closer to each other on the same level.

Not only does it assist the Finns in deliberation. At least one other important leader found the sauna invaluable in self-understanding. Canadian Prime Minister Pierre Elliott Trudeau, then sixty-four, trudged home alone in mid-March 1984 through a deep blizzard, took a sauna, and made up his mind. He resigned. Later he notified his own members of Parliament and the press. ". . . Now I feel this it the appropriate time for someone else to assume this challenge."

Though it might sound strange to Americans that Finn soldiers far away from home would build a sauna, or that diplomacy could be conducted inside its four walls, a little common sense helps doubters understand: taking a sauna, could be used in myriad ways.

Chapter Thirty-One

Finns Who Don't Like to Sauna

. . . And then they go into a shack that's filled with boiling rocks
Hot enough to sterilize an Iron Ranger's socks
And sit there till they steam out every sin and every foible
And then jump into a frozen lake and claim that it's enjoible —
But there was one, a shy young man, and although he was Finnish,
The joys of winter had, for him, long started to diminish.
He was a Finn, the only Finn, who would not take a sauna.
"It isn't that I can't," he said. "I simply do not wanna.
To jump into a frozen lake is not my fondest wish.
For just because I am a Finn don't mean that I'm a fish."
His friends said, "Come on, Toivo! Let's go out to Sunfish Lake!"
A Finn who don't take saunas? Why there must be some mistake.
But Toivo said, "There's no mistake. I know that I would freeze
In water colder than myself (98.6°)."
Garrison Keiler, "The Finn Who Would Not Take a Sauna"

Most people who have taken saunas over a long period of time enthuse about them. But somehow, the wonderful curative effects of a sauna don't convert everyone.

Garrison Keillor, one of Minnesota's favorite humorists, concerned himself with this very topic in the poem, "The Finn Who Would Not Take a Sauna." Though many hardy Iron Rangers of

181

Minnesota thrive in the bitter winters, Keillor reveals that one young Finn, Toivo, didn't appreciate those extremes:

Toivo staved off the demands of his friends, but when he fell in love with a Finn beauty, he had to prove his worthiness—and give the sauna a whirl. The excruciating and hilarious details of the entire poem are found in Keillor's book *We Are Still Married* (1989, Viking, New York).

Like the fictional Toivo, real-life Clara Carlson, of Brimson, Minnesota disliked the extremes of saunas. She said, "Personally, I did not like sauna. I never have. I could never stand the hot, humid air. Going to the sauna got to be a social event. You'd go to your neighbors. Us kids would probably go all in one, and I would always stay behind because I did not like a sauna. I never have.

"I remember my grandma washing my hair, and getting soap in my eyes. We had to dunk our head—there was no sprinkler or anything to wash, a faucet or anything. You just dunked your head into a bucket of water and we'd get soap in our eyes and cry."

Not every Finn enjoys the sauna, according to I. Vuori in "Healthy and Unhealthy Sauna Bathing" in *Annals of Clinical Research*, Vuori identified a variety of physical, medical and social reasons: headache, mild malaise, dizziness, and restless sleep as other unpleasant symptoms. These problems occur more commonly with inexperienced bathers and are often related to the intensity and duration of the heat exposure. Vuori strongly encourages all bathers to pay careful attention to their feelings if saunas are not pleasurable events.

Mayme Isaacson Rajala, of BigFork, Minnesota, had to do just that. She didn't care for saunas after she started getting headaches while taking them. "That wasn't the sauna's fault—it was my fault because I threw so much cold water on the rocks. If the sauna got too steamy and too hot, the next day I would have a headache. That would be Sunday, so sometimes I didn't even get to church. The headache would take its time, maybe two or three days. This started when I was nine or ten years old. And it was hard because it was the only way we could really wash up. So I still took a sauna, but I'd sit on the lower bench."

When L. M. Edelsward researched sauna beliefs in Lappeenranta, a small town in Finland, the overwhelming response to sauna was enthusiastic. Only four of the 218 in her study voiced irritation or apathy in response to her question: "How would your life be different without a sauna?"

One Finnish woman age forty-eight, wrote, "My life would be just as comfortable without the sauna. Perhaps even more comfortable. I hate an obligatory sauna during visits. If you don't go to the sauna and if you don't have a really acceptable reason for it, the host and hostess will be easily offended."

Others felt indifferent. One woman, age thirty-three, said, "The sauna is not indispensable to me." Another, age twenty-six, said, "It wouldn't be different, there just wouldn't be a sauna." The last person found other activities more interesting: "The sauna almost gets forgotten and is not much used when there is so much else to do."

There might be a few more people out there too shy to let their neighbors know that the sauna is not their greatest pleasure, whether for social, physical or medical reasons. While Toivo survived the experience, Keillor does not tell us if he grew to like saunas and continued taking them with his bride.

This bather doesn't look like he's having fun. Sauna owners often collect unique sauna art, such as this three-dimensional sauna carving by A. L. Koski of California.

Chapter Thirty-Two

Sex in the Sauna
SOME LIKE IT HOTTER

Sauna baths were also believed to be useful for improving virility.
Unknown Finnish writer.

One reason the sauna remained strong in Finland, while other countries outlawed their sweatbaths, was that Finns disallowed the very behaviors that created problems in other countries—alcohol, swearing, inappropriate behavior, and sex.

In Finland, families sauna together naked without any thoughts about sex. Mauri Haikola, of Oulu, Finland, writes in *The Finnish Sauna*, "Even though people are naked in sauna, Finns do not see anything sex-related in their sauna tradition. Massage parlours and other (sometimes sexual) services that often come with a public sauna in the red-light districts of big cities are unknown phenomena in Finland. Going to sauna naked with all your family is not at all perverted. Instead, the sauna tradition makes it natural and comfortable for children to learn about human body, and for parents to tell them about it."

While families sauna together, unmarried couples do not. According to Haikola, "Women used to give birth in saunas a long time ago, but the conceiving was done mostly elsewhere. Of course, you can have sex in there if you feel like it, but that is neither a part of any tradition nor very comfortable."

184

The sauna is sensual, but never sexual, in Finland. With narrow hard wooden benches and temperatures around 180 degrees F., the sauna was not designed for licentious activity. One misstep and the rocks will sear the skin. A cold dunk afterwards is the usual method prescribed to quell passion.

New World Order

When the sauna first arrived in the United States, the Finnish traditions stayed attached. The bathers knew the traditions and passed them on to their children. The invited neighbors followed the same customs as their hosts.

But when the sauna craze the United States in the 1960s and became a status, cultural translation was lost. New bathers didn't have neighbors to help them understand the tradition. Their information came from the newspapers, not the grandparents. So when people read of Finnish sweat bathing, they wondered, "Naked? In a warm dark room?" For some Americans, any nakedness equates to sex.

Perhaps the sex drive is increased and stimulated in the sauna bath, as Mikkel Aaland suggests. We know the brain is one of the human sex organs. Hillila quotes an old Chinese proverb, "In looking at anything, what is behind the eyes is at least as important as what is in front of the eyes." Maybe this is why the idea of sauna seems provocative to Americans.

Ask Gloria Jylka-Bishop's husband (now of Barnum, Minnesota): In the Air Force, he had been all over Europe—Denmark, Sweden, and other places where he had heard of saunas. But he had never been interested in taking one. When he came to meet his wife's family in Minnesota, he agreed he'd take a sauna. So Gloria went in with him. It was hot and congenial, and during the sauna they got even cozier. Afterwards he said to her, "If the sauna wasn't hot enough, then I had to make love to you, and it darned near killed me." Only the cold water he poured over himself cooled him off. Eventually he learned to like the actual sauna part of the experience.

"In the sauna everybody got clean," remembers Marvin Salo, of New York Mills, Minnesota. "They conceived children there too.

The Sami were very romantic. They wouldn't have sex if they weren't clean. Even when a husband died, the closest friend of the widow would go over and heat up her sauna, make her live again, and do this in a clear mind."

And speaking of romance, one woman even received a marriage proposal in the sauna. She was helping a very special young man to carry in wood. He abruptly popped the question, and she said yes. But until they were married, they didn't take saunas together.

Probably more than one couple lit the stove after they were in the sauna, and enjoyed sex while the sauna fire caught.

Chapter Thirty-Three

Saunas of the New Millenium

"I never met a sauna I didn't like."
Mark Raisanen of Saunatec, Inc.

People have all kinds of reasons for not getting a sauna. Here's what they say:

1. Electric heaters don't have enough rocks.
2. You can't throw water on the electric stoves.
3. Couples like different combinations of heat and humidity.
4. People don't want to build a sauna in a home if they have to move.
5. I get claustrophobic in a closed, dim box.
6. I get dizzy or headaches.
7. Saunas are too big.
8. They look dark and boxy in modern homes.
9. They cost too much.
10. They are too hard to build if you don't have carpentry skills.
11. The heater is dangerous and could burn you.
12. Electric stove controls are on the bottom and hard to reach.
13. The heater switch needs a time-delay starter.
14. We are allergic to pine, glues, and chemicals.
15. Wood benches cause splinters in embarrassing locations.
16. (Write your own here . . .)

An upscale sauna built with lots of glass in a small space (left) prevents claustrophobia. Custom-built saunas and sauna kits use high-quality materials (right) are available. (Photos from Saunatec, Inc.)

The people who manufacture saunas have been listening to those complaints and have developed saunas and stoves to meet every need. The variety in new saunas is amazing. Manufacturers continue to develop new products and refine solutions for current problems. How have they addressed the above concerns?

More Rocks, Please

The new generation of electric stoves uses more rocks. Since the rocks radiate gentle heat, the more rocks, the better it feels in the sauna. Although the ton that a *savusauna* used is not needed, fifty to seventy-five pounds will work wonders in the new stoves, which use quarried olivine and peridotite, (described more fully in Chapter 15). "Rocks should fill the heaters, top to bottom, says Mark Raisanen of Saunatec, Inc., in Cokato, Minnesota. "If your rocks just sit in a pan on top of the heater, your sauna will feel like a toaster. If you have had your sauna stove for a few years, and you can see the elements, add more rocks. "

After a few years, rocks will need to be replaced. But if the rocks are changed and different kinds (whether to match the decor or to commemorate your trip) are added, the warranty of the stove could be voided by not using the rocks for which the heaters were designed. Don't expect the heater company or Underwriters Laboratories to replace your stove.

The new electric stoves meet safety standards established by the Underwriters Laboratories. For example, the stainless steel grate on top has to pass a "towel test," which means that a towel won't burn if laid over the grate. Don't waste time testing this—the Underwriters Laboratories has already done it.

The heating elements and rocks are wrapped with up to three walls of stainless steel, insulating people from the heating elements and preventing burns to skin. Bathers who accidentally touch a heater while it's warming will notice the heat, but won't burn. This is a far cry from the open flames of the old saunas that frequently caused the whole building to burn down.

Safety to bathers is important. The new generation of sauna heaters uses triple-wall construction to prevent burns. It also offers large rock capacity for more comfortable steam. (Photo from Sauna-tec, Inc.)

It's the Humidity and the Heat

The engineers added a timer to turn the heater on when no one is around (one can be set up to twelve hours in advance). They moved control knobs to the side, where where they are easily visible and handy to adjust. State-of-the-art digital readouts are available, as well as light switch controls and indicator lights for the sauna heater.

People react to different levels of heat and moisture in the sauna. In the early years, electric stoves created such a hot and dry sauna experience that those who could chose wood-burning stoves with water-heating capabilities—a water tank on the side, or maybe a large bucket on top. As the stove heated, moisture entered the air. With electric stoves, for a long time that just wasn't possible.

Enter the engineers, who developed a steamier sauna, with a separate steam generator. It won't overheat or boil dry (as is possible with a bucket on a wood-burner if left too long unattended). With the separate steam generator, one can appreciate the kind of sauna prefers, one with high temperature and low humidity or one with lower temperatures and higher humidity.

An accessory to the heater, a Sauna Heart can deliver humidity. The Sauna Heart adds without throwing water on the rocks. Water fills a tube placed deep into the rocks. When heated, it bubbles up into a special cup at the top of the heater and onto the rocks themselves.

A Sauna for Everyone

Architects and designers have improved other features too. The Thera-Port, an instant sauna, comes in two pieces narrow enough to fit through a regular-size door. No new plumbing or finishing work is required. It can be set on any floor, locked together, plugged into a standard fifteen-amp outlet and ready to steam in maybe fifteen minutes, tops. When moving, the two sections unlock and load on the mover's truck. Just like that.

This portable sauna from Saunatec, Inc. (left), can be delivered through normal doorways in two pieces, locked together, and ready for heating in fifteen minutes. No plumbing needed. A pre-fab sauna (right) doesn't have to look like a clunky, dark box. This Sisu model has side windows. (Photos from Saunatec, Inc.)

A portable will fit one or two people. For a bigger sauna, architects have designed beautiful saunas, with clear white (non-staining) woods, soft lighting, and enough glass to make your bathroom or basement feel open and airy. The woods used today don't conduct heat, which means a cooler bench to sit or lean against. There is often a choice of woods to use, all of which can be non-allergenic and non-splintery.

Home builders can plan their own design or use a standard kit (available in many sizes). The prefabricated kits can be put together (with two people) in half a day. All the modules are numbered and the door is hung and mounted in its own panel. That's much easier than trying to build one from a book of instructions. Plus, with a standard kit comes the knowledge that the sauna has been carefully designed to include adequate ventilation. A sauna without proper ventilation can cause the bathers inside to feel ill, dizzy and headachy.

Upscale options, like etched-glass doors, an unusual shape, elegant woodwork, skylights or other windows — they are all easily available. These new saunas fit into all decor styles in both modern and older homes. Architects have created contemporary designs using more glass. In fact, a larger piece of glass in the door not only enables one to see out better, it actually stabilizes the door and helps prevent warping, so the door closes without sticking or leaving cracks.

There's a sauna available for every place of living, every lifestyle and most checkbooks.

This Skyline Sauna features a geometric front window wall. (Photo from Saunatec, Inc.)

This Elysee Designer series features a six-sided design with angular sidelite windows and could be incorporated into master suites. (Photo from Saunatec, Inc.)

The newest designer sauna, the Moonlight, from Saunatec, Inc., has a broad-angled front. Adding a steam suite converts the bathroom into a luxury spa. (Photo from Saunatec, Inc.)

191

The Alpha and the Omega

Different kinds, styles, and sizes of saunas have been used throughout history, more have been developed in the past ten years, and even more and different ones will be created in the future. But the core reasons for taking a sauna — health, a sense of well-being, cama-raderie, and a host of other positive reasons — have never changed.

Ponder that when plopping down on the sauna bench, as water dribbles on the rocks and *löyly* gently massages the muscles. The sauna is a link with history, the concept unchanged from the time a millenia ago, when Lasse dropped his cup full of tea on the hot stones in that covered hut dug into the half-frozen side of the hill, until today.

Bibliography

Books

Aaland, Mikkel. *Sweat.* Santa Barbara: Capra Press, 1978.

Annals of Clinical Research. Vol 20, No. 4, Special Issue on the Sauna. Helsinki, Finland: The Finnish Medical Society Duodecim, 1988.

Bruchac, Joseph. *The Native American Sweat Lodges: History and Legends.* Freedom, California: The Crossing Press, 1997.

Children of the Finnish Homestead Oral History Project. Stone, Joann Hanson. Chisholm, Minnesota: Iron Range Research Center, Ironworld Discovery Center, 1994.

Dal Maso, Leonardo B. *Rome of the Caesars.* Firenze: Bonechi-Edizion, 1976.

Edelsward, L.M. *Sauna as Symbol.* New York: Peter Lang Publishing, 1993.

Hillila, Bernhard. *The Sauna Is....* Iowa City, Iowa: Penfield Press, 1988.

Hollander, Carlton. *How to Build a Sauna.* New York: Sterling Publishing, 1978.

Johnson, Amandus. *The Swedish Settlements on the Delaware.* Volume 1. New York: Burt Franklin, 1970.

Johnson, Tom and Miller, Tim. *The Sauna Book.* New York: Harper and Row, 1977.

The Kalevala, *or Poems of the* Kalevala *District,* compiled by Elias Lonnrot, Maguon, Francis Peabody Jr., translation. Cambridge, Massachetts: Harvard University Press, 1975.

The Kalevala: *Epic of the Finnish People.* Friberg, Eino, translation. Helsinki Finland: Otava Publishing, 1988.

Rajanen, Aini. *Of Finnish Ways.* Minneapolis: Dillon Press, 1981.

Sauna Studies. Papers Read at the VI International Congress. Teir, Harald, Yrjo Collan and Pirkko Valtakari, eds. Helsinki, Finland: Suomen Saunaseura, 1976.

Viherjuuri, H. J. *Sauna: The Finnish Bath.* Brattleboro, Vermont: Stephen Green Press, 1965.

Virtanen, John O. *The Finnish Sauna: Peace of Mind, Body and Soul.* Withee, Wisconsin: OW Enterprise, 1998.

Magazine Articles

Gagliardi, Nancy. "Serious Soothers: Tired Muscles and Skin Deserve Post Workout Pampering." *Working Woman.* June 1985: 38.

Li, Leslie. "Taking the Heat." *Health.* January 1990: 62.

Paulson, Barbara. "Sweat." *Health.* July-August 1994:94.

Pearce, Richard. "Sauna Vs. Steam." *Shape.* February 1997:86-88, 117-118.

Tanny, Armand. "Sweat it! A Sauna Update." *Muscle and Fitness.* October 1998: 202-205.

Tanny, Armand. "A Soothing Sauna." *Muscle and Fitness.* May 1996: 192-195.

Internet

Aaland, Mikkel. *Sweat.* <http://www.cyberbohemia.com/Pages/sweat.htm>

Bird, Tim. "Letting off Steam, the Finnish Way," *Blue Wings* <http//www.hut.fi~icankar/sauna/bluew.html>

Cankar, Mihael. <http//www.hut.fi~icankar/sauna/index.htm> (a multitude of articles and links)

"The Farmer, the Devil and the Sauna," *Sauna Lore.* <http//www.sauna.org/lore-farrmer.html>

The Finnish Sauna Society. <http//www.sauna.fi>

Haikola, Mauri. "4.6 The Finnish Sauna." *Nordic FAQ.* <http//www.landfield.com/faq/nordic-faq/part4_FINLAND/section-5.html>

Laaksonen, Pekka. "The Sauna as a National Symbol." *Virtual Finland.* <http//www.vn.fi/vn/um/finfo/english/sauna.html>

Norros, Mikko. "Bare Facts of the Sauna" *Virtual Finland.* <http//www.vn.fi/vn/um/finfo/english/saunajuttu.html>

The Sauna Site. <http//www.saunasite.com>

"Soumalienen Sauna: The Finnish Sauna and Log House" *Finnish Sauna Culture* <http//www.geodities.com/Athens/Parthenon/3818/SAUNA.HTM>

"An Age-Old Fountain of Youth." *Steam Therapy News* <http//www.siouxlan.com/spas/sauna/news/steamtherapy1.html>

"Magical Mists," *Steam Therapy News* <http//www.siouxlan.com/spas/sauna/news/steamtherapy2.html>

The Ice Sauna 2000 <wysiwyg://8/http://www.geocities.com/Athens/Acropolis/1895/jaas2000.html>

Resources

Saunatec Inc.
575 E. Cokato Street
Cokato, MN 55321
800-346-6536

Kangas Sauna
379 Oliver Road
Thunder Bay, Ontario   P7B 2G1
Canada
Open 7 days a week, year-round
807-344-6761

Ely Steam Bath
Richard Ahola
Ely, MN
218-365-6728
Open Wednesday and Friday
(3:30-8:30) and Saturday (1:30-8:30)

Rozycki Manufacturing
Superior Cooperage
P.O.Box 128
Rice, MN
320-393-2444

Ironworld Discovery Center
Iron Range Research Center
P.O. Box 392
Chisholm, MN 55719-0392
800-372-6437
http://www.ironworld.com

Scandanavian Heritage Park
Minot, ND

Mealey's Gift and Sauna Shop
124 N. Central
Ely, MN 55731
218-365-3639

Conga Se Menne
Les Ross
P.O. Box 48
Negaunee, MI 49866
906-475-9399
http://www.congaonline.com